FOREWORD

Countless people of all ages in Britain are now taking an interest in wild birds. More often than not this interest arises in the first place from contact with birds in gardens and parks. This is fine in itself and one of the attractions of birds is that we can enjoy them during short breaks in our everyday humdrum existence. I welcome this book as it will give an opportunity for this early interest to be widened and deepened and to include some of the more unusual species. It can point the way to broader horizons.

As pressures on land increase, the importance of nature reserves for safeguarding our wild birds increases also. They are the foundation of our practical achievements in conservation and have particular value for rarer and more sensitive species. The authors fully appreciate and demonstrate this and in addition show how at the same time, without any detriment to the birds or habitat, reserves can provide enormous pleasure. Some of the best bird country is also some of the most scenically rewarding and the authors have thoughtfully included nearby places of historic interest.

The book reveals the long and deep interest in wild birds held by both authors. The combination of Robert Dougall's skill as a commentator and as a former President of the Royal Society for the Protection of Birds with Herbert Axell's experience of reserve management, and latterly as the Society's Land Use Adviser, guarantees an informative and extremely readable volume. Robert Gillmor's line drawings are as always a delight. This is very much a book for all the family and should also be of value to visitors from overseas. Above all, this book may for many serve as an introduction to a new and abiding leisure interest.

IAN PRESTT

BIRDWATCH ROUND BRITAIN

BIRDWATCH ROUND BRITAIN

with
ROBERT DOUGALL
and
HERBERT AXELL

A Personal selection of
Britain's Bird Reserves

Foreword by Ian Prestt

Director of
the Royal Society for the Protection of Birds

COLLINS and HARVILL PRESS
14 St James's Place, London

William Collins Sons & Co Ltd
London · Glasgow · Sydney · Auckland
Toronto · Johannesburg

British Library Cataloguing in Publication Data

Dougall, Robert
  Birdwatch round Britain with Robert Dougall and Herbert Axell.
  1. Bird watching—Great Britain
  I. Title   II. Axell, Herbert
  598.2′073′0941   QL677.5

ISBN 0-00-262256-4

Line drawings by Robert Gillmor
Maps by Brian and Constance Dear

First published 1982
© Robert Dougall and Herbert Axell 1982
Photo set in Garamond
Made and Printed in Great Britain by
William Collins Sons & Co Ltd Glasgow

This book is dedicated to
all wardens of bird reserves —
key men in
the conservation of birdlife

CONTENTS

PLATES
Between pages 96 and 97

Knots on the Dee Estuary during winter
Guillemots, Kittiwakes and Shags, Inner Farne
Kittiwakes and Guillemots, Papa Westray, Orkney
Hermaness 'Bird City', Shetland
Loch Garten, Inverness
'The Neck', Skomer Island, South West Wales
Bempton Cliffs, Yorkshire
Heronry at Northward Hill, Kent
Holkham Marshes, Norfolk
Hickling Broad, Norfolk
Leighton Moss, Lancashire
Minsmere, Suffolk

MAPS

LINE DRAWINGS

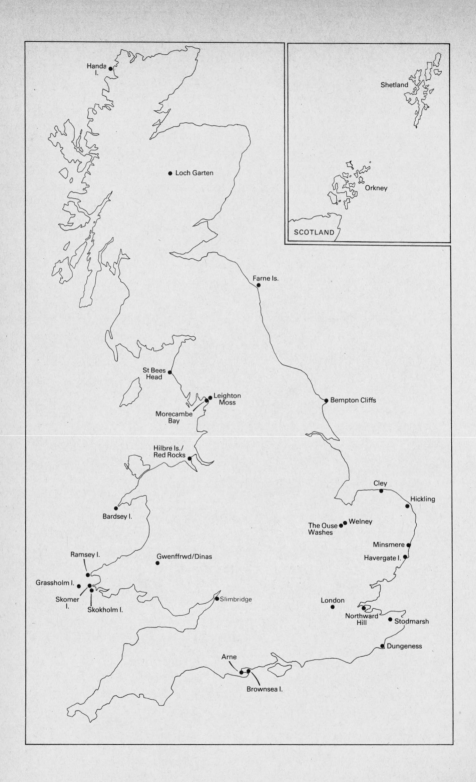

INTRODUCTION

Birdwatching has now become the fastest growing leisure activity in many countries and especially in Britain. The membership of the Royal Society for the Protection of Birds has soared to well over 350,000, which makes it by far the most important voluntary conservation body in Europe. The Society owns, or manages, some eighty reserves covering about 90,000 acres dispersed over the length and breadth of the British Isles. There are in addition many other conservation bodies managing bird reserves – among them the Wildfowl Trust, the network of County Naturalists' Trusts, the Nature Conservancy Council and the National Trusts.

To someone coming new to this interest, the multiplicity of organizations and reserves can seem confusing. We have therefore written this book in an attempt to simplify the scene by making a personal selection of what, in our opinion, are the most rewarding of the reserves. Those included have all been personally visited recently by one, or in most cases, by both of us.

Realizing that countless people now place bird interest high on their list of priorities when making holiday plans, we have also described the settings of the individual reserves in terms of more general recreational interest.

Finally we should like to express our thanks to all the reserve wardens, to Tom Slack, an RSPB Council Member, and, in particular, to John Parslow, RSPB Director (Conservation), who kindly read the manuscript; also to Marjorie Villiers and Hilary Davies for their invaluable editorial guidance.

Above all our thanks go to the Director of the RSPB, Ian Prestt, for kindly agreeing to write the Foreword and to Michèle Byam, whose idea this book was.

ROBERT DOUGALL
HERBERT AXELL

CHAPTER ONE

London

Most visitors to London probably know the wartime song about the Nightingale in Berkeley Square, but may not realize that the capital today, in addition to its other much publicized attractions, is in fact an excellent place for birding. It is also as good a place as any from which to begin our clockwise tour of selected British bird reserves.

For birdlife, London has the tremendous advantage of being the greenest of all the world's capital cities: its urban jungle has many clearings comprising a wide variety of habitats. In addition to the Royal Parks, there are countless residential squares and gardens, reservoirs, gravel pits, docks, sewage farms, rubbish tips and, of course, the River Thames. Church spires and even tower-blocks are used for roosting and nesting by some former rock- and cliff-dwelling birds. Above all, London can offer relative safety, warmth and food.

The days are happily gone when bird-trappers used to ply their trade in the London parks; and when youths thought nothing of taking potshots from trains at song-birds perched on telegraph wires. Less than 100 years ago, when gulls first began to fly up the Thames, they were often greeted with a murderous barrage of lead-shot from the bridges. Today, especially in winter, they can be seen patrolling everywhere as welcome visitors and the only barrage they meet is of bread.

Gone too are the Dickensian pea-soup fogs and the omnipresent coating of grime on buildings and foliage. This cleaner air has helped some of the insectivorous birds to return to central London: the Robin and the Spotted Flycatcher are the most successful, and House Martins have raised young high up on a tall building near Hyde Park Corner. Swallows, Lesser Whitethroats and Goldcrests have nested in Regent's Park. Sand Martins are frequently seen.

The numbers of the rare Black Redstart have now built up to at least thirty pairs. This soot-coloured bird with a fiery tail did not breed in Britain at all until 1923 when two pairs nested in Sussex. Gradually, it moved into central London and in 1940 succeeded in raising two broods in the precincts of Westminster Abbey. Soon Hitler's blitz was providing plenty of rubble and wasteland rich with insects. The 'firetails' quickly made themselves at home in all kinds of industrial situations and by 1973 one was even heard giving a staccato warble inside a jumbo-jet hangar at Heathrow Airport.

It is a bonus for waterfowl that the Thames is again relatively clean in a remarkable transformation carried out over the past twenty years or so. The stage had been reached when only the Common Eel and one or two other hardy species of fish were able to survive in the heavily polluted water; today, there are ninety-seven different species and there is hope that salmon may one day be seen leaping under Westminster Bridge, as they did not much more than a century ago.

So, thanks to the improved conditions following the series of Bird Protection Acts, the Clean Air Act of 1956 and the purification of the river, there can be seen today, within a 5-mile radius of St Paul's, some 110 species of wild birds; and about half that number stay to breed.

The two great bird survivors in even the most densely built-over areas are the House Sparrow and the Feral Pigeon. Both are well able to exist as scavengers almost anywhere in London – even on some stations of the underground railway. Nevertheless, the House Sparrow population has declined steeply with the departure of horse traffic from the streets. Next to them in number come Woodpigeons, Starlings and, in winter, Black-headed Gulls.

One of London's greatest bird spectacles is the mass roosting of Starlings on buildings, especially around Trafalgar Square. From early autumn onward, the evening air is filled with their shrill screaming as flock after flock pour in from the countryside to settle like a black fringe along cornices and window ledges where they stand packed shoulder to shoulder.

Starlings are less dependent on man for food than House Sparrows and may fly each day up to 30 miles along well-defined flight lines to fields and open places where they forage for insects and grubs. The vast roosts not only provide warmth and security, but may also have their uses as information centres, where knowledge can be exchanged of the best feeding grounds.

Foremost among central London's unique heritage of open spaces are the Royal Parks. Many of them are centrally situated in the West End: an almost continuous belt of green runs from St James's Park across Green Park to Hyde Park and Kensington Gardens. The small woodland areas of Holland Park and Fulham Palace Gardens are also close. To the northwest lie Regent's Park and Primrose Hill; to the south Battersea Park; in the east Southwark Park and Victoria Park in Hackney.

The largest of these is Regent's Park, comprising 472 acres with large stretches of water and some island sanctuaries. On one of the wooded islets there has been a breeding colony of wild Herons since 1968. This has now built up to at least eight or nine pairs; the only objectors are some of the residents of neighbouring St John's Wood, who find their goldfish ponds mysteriously emptied. Regent's Park is also, of course, the home of the London Zoo, and one of these great grey birds regularly attends at feeding time for the sea-lions. As 3.30 p.m. approaches, a lone, gaunt figure is seen high up on a building overlooking the rocky pool. With impeccable timing he descends in ungainly fashion to snatch at least one glinting mackerel, before it can be scooped up by a floundering seal. This solitary hunter of the fens has adapted well to life in town.

Herons are also often seen along the banks of the Serpentine in Hyde Park; and in both these parks four or five pairs of Great Crested Grebes regularly nest. These richly adorned water birds have a primitive reptilian grace, and this distinction very nearly caused their extermination in Britain in the latter part of the last century. In those days, grand ladies wore vast hats like mausoleums of dead birds, and grebe plumes were in great demand. The downy feathers from the white satinlike breast were also used as a cosy lining for muffs. Eventually, only forty-two pairs of the elegant birds remained in the whole country.

The formation of the Society for the Protection of Birds in 1889 was instrumental in helping to save them. It received the Royal Charter in 1904. One of the rules was that lady-members must 'refrain from wearing the feathers of any bird not killed for the purposes of food, the Ostrich only excepted'. Legislation to control the plumage trade followed, and it is thanks to this that today we can see these splendid birds, once confined to remote Scottish lochs, in several of the London parks. Their spread has been greatly helped by the flooded gravel pits and the network of huge reservoirs around the capital, which have provided ideal breeding places.

It is an exceptional privilege now to be able to watch their spectacular and complex courtship displays. First, they swim towards each other, chestnut and black tippets spread like frills about their heads. They touch bills gently and with the help of their lobed toes the birds rise to full height – standing almost upright on the water. They then sink down again with heads drawn back and move slightly apart. Vigorous head-shaking follows and the upward stretching is repeated.

Another ritual ceremony concerns the gathering and presentation of water weed by each bird. They dash towards each other and just before meeting rise to full height, almost breast to breast, with the weed dangling down between them. This is the prelude to setting about the job of choosing a site for a mating platform. The Grebes are splendid parents and for much of the first few weeks the tiny zebra-striped chicks climb on to their parents' backs where, cradled among feathers, they are safe from pike and other predators. It is fully two months before they are independent and, in the meantime, a high-pitched cheeping is sustained while the ever solicitous parents dive and dive again to satisfy the insatiable demand for fish. There are few more fascinating wildlife spectacles than the intimate family life of these strangely beautiful water birds.

In addition, most of the Royal Parks have some introduced

waterfowl and there are officially-recognized collections in St James's Park and in Regent's Park. By far the oldest is the one in St James's Park. James I used to keep a menagerie there, including 'outlandish fowl' such as 'Cassowaries and Cormorants'. Today Cormorants are still present and another traditional fowl is the Pelican: the Czar of Russia first presented a pair to Charles II and Pelicans remain a popular feature of the park. In the collection itself there are some 200 ducks and about 40 geese.

The collection at Regent's Park has 70 or so ducks from twenty-four species and about 26 geese from eight species. These are mostly pinioned, but each year they are joined by hundreds of free-flying birds such as Mallard, Pochard, Tufted Duck and the striking, but over-successful, Canada Geese, which in some places are having to be controlled.

The largest of all the Royal Parks is a few miles southwest at Richmond-on-Thames, where Charles I used to hunt. Herds of the magnificent Red and the dainty Fallow Deer still roam through the woods and bracken. The park covers well over 2000 acres and has several wooded sanctuaries set among undulating grassland with clumps of ancient oaks. Here, more than 100 species of wild birds are seen each year and about 60 stay to breed. Among rarities seen on or near Pen Ponds in recent years have been a Black-necked Grebe in summer plumage and a Great Grey Shrike which stayed throughout one winter. Goldeneye, Curlew, Kittiwake, Bearded Reedling, Pied Flycatcher and White Wagtail have also been present from time to time and, in 1975, Water Rail and Grey Wagtail were recorded as breeding at Richmond for the first time.

In general, all the London parks continue to attract birds in ever greater diversity. There are fewer House Sparrows and Starlings and big increases in Blackbirds, Woodpigeons, Carrion Crows and Tufted Ducks. Among the newer breeding birds are Coot, Magpie, Jay, Redpoll, Goldcrest and Long-tailed Tit.

Kestrels now nest on buildings and church spires in many parts of the capital. Like the Crows, they doubtless find a welcome absence of gamekeepers and there are plenty of Sparrows and rodents for food. An important asset for the 'windhover' in adapting to city life is its manoeuvrability and mastery of flight. In a crowded scene it can pin-point its prey and descend to grab it with a precision a helicopter pilot might envy. One was spotted recently in leisurely flight behind Harrods, until a Pied Wagtail attacked it from the rear, twittering furiously and forcing it to peel off towards Brompton Road and possibly Hyde Park. The wagtail may well have been one of the 300 or so Pied Wagtails which have a winter roost in a small plane tree in the middle of busy Hammersmith Broadway.

The Tawny Owls, too, have taken to London and at dusk in winter near the parks an eerie duet can sometimes be heard. The male gives a long-drawn-out, hollow-sounding hoot and the female's shrill 'kee-wick', in reply, hangs like a whip-lash on the frosty air.

In addition to the Royal Parks, central London has important 'lungs' around the perimeter. Among these 3500 acres of commons and heaths are Wimbledon Common, Putney Heath, Blackheath and the famous Hampstead Heath, which is the most rural of them all. Only 5 miles from the centre, its 850 acres on the northern heights give a spacious feel of unspoilt country unequalled in any of the world's great cities. Hampstead can offer a marvellous variety of scene: there are hints of the downs by the sea, of moorland, marsh and woodland – all in exquisite union. It attracts over 40 species of breeding birds, including all three British woodpeckers, the Great Spotted, the Lesser Spotted occasionally, and always the Green. All told, about ninety species are recorded most years, often including such shy birds as Water Rails and Snipe.

There is no doubt that the capital's birdlife has benefited enormously from the extensive chain of reservoirs running across the north of Greater London. Two of the best are at Staines and Barn Elms. At Staines no permit is required and there is excellent viewing, from a public causeway. Here are regular flocks of Goldeneye, Goosander and Smew, also the occasional Long-tailed Duck, Red-breasted Merganser or Pintail. In November 1979 an official Wildfowl Count gave figures of 5000 Pochard and 4000 Tufted Duck – numbers which would do credit to a Scottish loch. The reservoirs are also of especial interest during migration when Greenshank, Black-necked Grebe, Common and Arctic Terns, as well as Black Terns, are frequently seen. Yellow Wagtails breed regularly at Staines.

At the Walthamstow group of reservoirs there is the fifth largest heronry in Britain, numbering about 100 pairs. Some trees hold three or four nests and the overcrowding has probably led to the birds spreading out to form the small colony in Regent's Park.

Another indication of the adaptability of birds came when the Surrey Docks on the south side of the Thames were closed in 1970. The disused land quickly attracted a goodly variety and even produced the first breeding records for Inner London of Red-legged Partridge, Lapwing, Ringed and Little Ringed Plovers, Skylark and Reedbunting.

For dedicated birdwatchers there are also numerous sewage works and rubbish tips. There is even one fine sludge-settling bed near the runways on the western edge of Heathrow Airport. This artificial marsh is an ideal stopping-off place for the globe-trotting waders on their great migration flights between Africa and the far north.

And then, of course, there are the cemeteries, which also make marvellous refuges for birds – Highgate and Brompton are two of the best.

It may seem odd to think of London as a vast wild bird sanctuary, but then, as Dr Johnson once propounded: 'when a man is tired of London, he is tired of life; for there is in London all that life can afford.'

For more detailed information refer to the Ornithological Section of the London Natural History Society, c/o British Museum, Cromwell Road, London, SW7. Tel: (01)-589 6323. Field outings are organized in and around London.

Permits to visit reservoirs from: The Divisional Manager, Metropolitan Water Division, New River Head, Rosebery Avenue, London EC1R 4TP. Tel: (01)-837 3300 Ext. 2418. The applicant must be 18 or over and preferably a member of an ornithological society. For Staines Reservoir no permit is required.

A leaflet on birdwatching at reservoirs can be obtained from the Regional Amenity Officer, Thames Water, Nugent House, Vastern Road, Reading RG1 8DB. Tel: Reading 593538. An SAE should be enclosed with the request.

For members of the RSPB there are ten London Groups which organize field outings in and around the capital. Details from RSPB, The Lodge, Sandy, Bedfordshire SG19 2DL. Tel: (0767)-80551.

CHAPTER TWO

Brownsea Island, Dorset
National Trust/Dorset Naturalists' Trust

This beautiful island sanctuary lies within the narrow entrance of Poole Harbour, as a pushed-in cork floats in the neck of a bottle. The harbour itself is like an inland sea with a broken shoreline extending for nearly 100 miles; yet access to it is through a stretch of water only a few hundred yards wide. There is no bridge, just a car-ferry, so most through-traffic keeps away and passes well to the north. Certainly, Brownsea, although surrounded by one of Britain's most popular holiday areas, has managed to retain its natural beauty of woods, heaths, lakes and marshes.

It is now an important reserve for birds, with some 200 species recorded – of which 65 have bred, more than 60 of them regularly. Although only 1½ miles long and ¾ mile wide, it has seen a great deal of history and is the largest and best-known of the islands in the haven.

Set in summer for the most part among blue waters, the name of Brownsea may seem puzzling. It derives from the Old English 'Brunkeseye': eye stems from 'ieg', the word for an island. The first syllable may come from 'brunc' meaning a steep hill, or possibly from 'Brunoc' – a man's name.

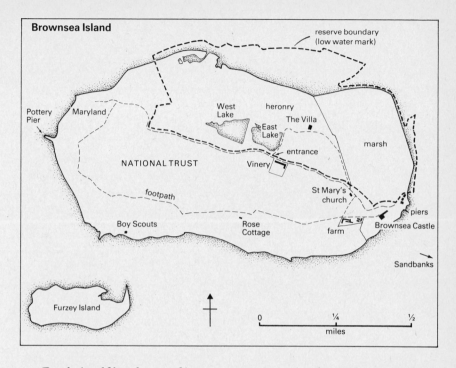

Poole itself has been of importance since the days of King Alfred and his first English fleet. Canute and his rampaging Danes stormed ashore here; probably Richard the Lionheart set sail for the Crusades from the harbour, and even in the last war it was the scene of momentous comings and goings as a terminus for flying-boats from all over the world. Poole is now a large residential and holiday centre, stretching away to the east as far as the borders of Bournemouth; for yachtsmen Poole Harbour is unequalled.

Brownsea has shared in all its history: here Henry VIII built a square gun-fort to defend the harbour and, over the centuries, this has been considerably enlarged as a castle, destroyed by fire and then rebuilt. For hundreds of years monks resided on the island. The first exploitation of the island's resources came in the 17th century when, among other things, clay was extracted for making pottery and tobacco pipes. In the 18th and 19th centuries yet more clay was needed for industrial earthenware; during this period St Mary's Church was built and a hamlet called Maryland came into being. The old vicarage has now become the reserve headquarters and is named 'The Villa'.

Fortunately for the island's wildlife, successive owners, for the most part, behaved with great responsibility and introduced a considerable variety of trees and shrubs. In the southwest corner of the island one of Brownsea's chief claims to fame is commemorated by a stone: this tells how in 1907 it became the birthplace of the worldwide Boy Scout Movement when Sir Robert Baden-Powell held his first scout camp here.

Twenty years later, there came a turning-point in the careful management of the estate, when a new owner refused to allow any interference or control whatever with nature. Soon, inevitably, a wilderness developed of rhododendron, laurel and bamboo tangled with dense scrub from the pine and birch woods.

Finally, in 1962, Brownsea was handed over to the National Trust and 240 acres of the northern half of the island were leased to the Dorset Naturalists' Trust. The light-blocking jungle was removed, a wider variety of plants and vegetation reappeared and wildlife soon recovered. The woods now hold one of the largest heronries in Britain with, in a good year, 110 pairs of the great grey birds.

Many small, woodland song-birds breed here including Goldcrests, Treecreepers and Blackcaps. Sparrowhawks nest, as do Green and Great Spotted Woodpeckers and Woodcock. The very rare Dartford Warblers and Nightjars nest on the heath; Reed and Sedge Warblers and Reed Buntings in the freshwater reed marsh and around the two small lakes. In addition, Peacocks and four species of pheasant, including the spectacular Golden, are able to breed in the wild, thanks to the absence of Foxes. Among the resident water birds are Water Rails, Little Grebes and Tufted Duck.

The greatest concentration of birds can be seen on the 70-acre salt-water lagoon, from three hides, one of them open free to the public. Among the breeding birds are 110 pairs of Sandwich Terns, about 100 Common Terns and Herring Gulls, a variable number of Black-headed Gulls, many Shelducks and small numbers of Oystercatchers and Canada Geese. There was a noteworthy event in 1977 when a pair of Snow Geese, which had escaped from a collection, bred for the first time here in the wild. When the feeding areas in Poole Harbour are covered at high-tide, this quiet stretch of controlled shallow water, mudflats and artificially constructed shingle islands attracts hundreds of migrant and wintering waders, including Curlew, Whimbrel, Godwits, Grey Plover, Greenshank and about twelve Avocets.

Offshore, around the island, outside the breeding season, rare Slavonian, Black-necked and Red-necked Grebes may be seen with a variety of ducks including Goldeneye. At first glance, the Goldeneye drake appears black and white, and a round white patch behind the bill shows up clearly, even in flight. If he should allow a closer inspection, his large head is seen to have a dark green metallic sheen, which dramatically sets off the jewel-like, golden eye.

There are only a few species of mammals on Brownsea and the most important of them is the Red Squirrel. On the mainland most of its territory has now been taken over by the more predatory North American Grey.

There are also many moths and butterflies including the White Admiral.

Access By ferry from Poole Quay or Sandbanks. Boats run hourly between 10 a.m. and 5 p.m.
Opening times Open all year.
Facilities Suitable for all the family. National Trust Information Office at Town Quay landing place. This has a restaurant and shop. On the island, Dorset Naturalists' Trust runs an Information Centre and shop. Here nature trail leaflets are available. The Trust runs guided tours of the reserve daily at 2.30 p.m. from 1 April to 30 September. St Mary's Church (1853) has many fine carved figures. Mooring for dinghies at New Pottery Pier at west end of the island, where there is good bathing.
Warden National Trust, Brownsea Island, Poole, Dorset.
Dorset Naturalists' Trust Nature Reserve, The Villa, Brownsea Island, Poole, Dorset.

CHAPTER THREE

Arne Reserve, Dorset
RSPB

The RSPB now owns the freehold of more than 1100 acres of the Arne Peninsula, one of Dorset's last great heaths, at the western edge of Poole Harbour. This is of considerable importance as southern heathland has been steadily dwindling during this century and especially over the past twenty years or so. The main losses have been due to agricultural usage, extensive afforestation, building development and, to a lesser degree, mining for minerals. Up to 1960, Dorset still had 25,000 acres of heath. Today, only about half that amount remains and the sections are considerably fragmented and isolated from each other. This enhances the significance of Arne.

The reserve is notable as a traditional breeding place of one of Britain's rarest birds: the Dartford Warbler. The handsome male has a grey head, with dark brown upper parts and wine-red breast. With luck it may be possible to catch a glimpse of him in the breeding season when he shows himself on the tops of gorse bushes, long tail held cocked and keeping a wary look-out with his orange-red eyes. The female is slightly browner and even more difficult to see.

Although found in most counties south of the Thames up to fifty years ago, the bird is now in danger of extinction. The loss of

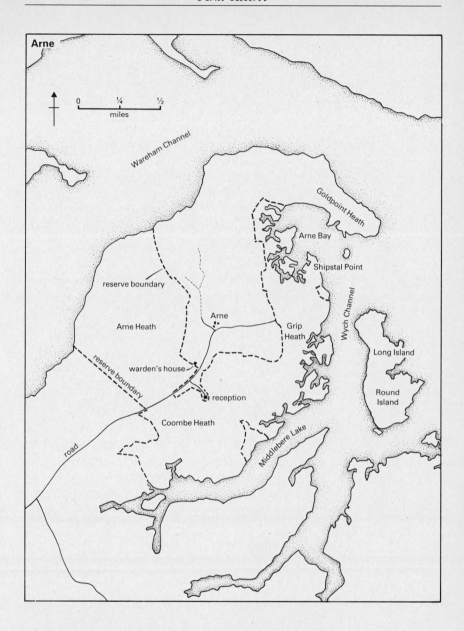

heathland, gorse fires and hard winters have greatly reduced its numbers. In any case it is on the edge of its breeding range in Britain: other members of its race are far more secure in the warmer

Mediterranean climate. For some reason, unlike other warblers, it chooses to stay with us throughout the winter and this can have a disastrous effect on its numbers. After the big freeze of 1963 only eleven pairs were known to have survived in Britain. Then, thanks to mild winters, the numbers built up again until by the early 1970s there were at least 300 pairs in Dorset and 30 of those on the Arne reserve. Then came the prolonged drought of 1976 which set the tinder-dry gorse and heather ablaze. Again there were bad winters in 1978 and 1979, until by the spring of the latter only two pairs of Arne's Dartford Warblers remained alive. By the following year there were four pairs, but it is no wonder that this handsome, unobtrusive little bird has now come to symbolize the whole problem of the conservation of southern England's heathland.

Another of Arne's birds is also under threat and difficult to see, although its strange, churring love-song may often be heard on warm, windless nights over the heath. The Nightjar is a bird of mystery and legend: Aristotle wrote that it sucked the udders of she-goats, which were then said to go blind. Even today, in some parts of the country, the bird is known as the Goat-sucker. In fact, the only reason for a Nightjar to haunt a goat yard would be to feast on the insects. In daytime, the bird lies motionless on the ground, confident that the marvellous camouflage of its plumage will make it almost invisible. At dusk the Nightjar leaves its hiding place to hunt moths and other flying insects by trapping them in its huge gaping bill.

More than fifty other species breed on Arne: the heath birds include Stonechats, Meadow Pipits, Linnets and Yellowhammers; in the woods there are Green Woodpeckers, Sparrowhawks and Goldcrests. Outside the breeding season, a wide variety of waders can be seen near the harbour. Large numbers of Black-tailed Godwits are present in early spring; also grebes and wildfowl during the winter.

Animals at Arne include Roe Deer and there are all six species of British reptiles including those rarities the Smooth Snake and Sand Lizard.

Close by, 4 miles southeast of Wareham, are the majestic ruins of Corfe Castle still dominating a gap in the Purbeck Hills. A castle has stood here since Saxon times: King Edward (the Martyr) is said to have been murdered within its walls in 978. The great stone tower was added more than 100 years later. During the Civil War, the castle was in the hands of the King's supporters, but a traitor in the garrison allowed Cromwell's Roundheads to break in. They finally blew it up with gunpowder in 1646. The village at the foot of the hill was very largely built of the grey Purbeck stone from the ruined castle.

In addition to the reserve, the most accessible birdwatching sites are in the bays of the north and east shores of Poole Harbour. Although the harbour itself is increasingly used for sailing and sport, it remains, despite all the disturbance, an important refuge for migrant and wintering waterfowl including Great Crested, Black-necked and Slavonian Grebes, Red-breasted Mergansers and many other sea ducks. Curlew and Black-tailed Godwits figure prominently in early spring together with a few Bar-tailed Godwits, Goldeneye and many other wildfowl and waders.

Access From the A351 Wareham road. A footpath from Arne village, 3 miles from Wareham, leads to Shipstal Point. (This is a good place to see waders and ducks on the mudflats and saltings.)
Opening times From the beginning of April to the end of August on Wednesdays, Thursdays, Saturdays and Sundays: from November to March on first and third Thursday and Sunday in each month. Shipstal Point area is open all year.
Permits In advance only from the Permit Secretary, 'Syldata', Arne, Wareham, Dorset BH20 5BT.
Facilities Suitable for all the family. A nature trail from Shipstal Point is open from the end of May to early September.
Warden 'Syldata', Arne, Dorset BH20 5BT.

CHAPTER FOUR

Slimbridge, Gloucestershire
Wildfowl Trust

Since it was set up in 1946, the Wildfowl Trust and the name Slimbridge have become internationally famous. Under its founder and director, Sir Peter Scott, it has won a worldwide reputation as a sanctuary for waterfowl, a wetland aviary and a research centre especially concerned with the survival of endangered species.

Here, on the eastern shore of the Severn Estuary in Gloucestershire the general public and members of the Trust can always be sure of seeing plenty of birds. The collection alone comprises 3000 birds and, with 131 of the 148 species of wildfowl represented, it is the largest and most varied in the world. The attractively landscaped enclosures of pens, lakes and paddocks extend over 100 acres and are surrounded by 1000 acres of farm-land and saltmarsh. This provides a secure feeding ground for numerous wild birds, many of which are doubtless attracted by the evident good living of the residents. Sir Peter with good reason has described Slimbridge as the largest bird feeding-table in the world.

The best time of all to visit the Wildfowl Trust headquarters is from late October until early March. It is then that the saltmarsh and

Slimbridge

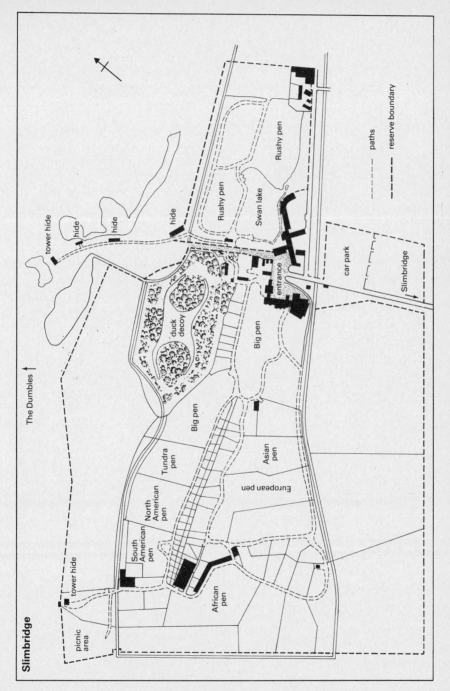

tower hide

hide

hide

hide

The Dumbles

duck decoy

Rushy pen

Swan lake

Rushy pen

entrance

Big pen

Big pen

Tundra pen

North American pen

South American pen

tower hide

picnic area

African pen

European pen

Asian pen

car park

Slimbridge

- - - - - paths

- - - - - reserve boundary

estuary become a wintering place for many thousands of geese, duck and waders. This stretch of wetland is known as the Dumbles and it draws a great gathering of wildfowl. Most numerous are the European White-fronted Geese, which fly in each year from their Arctic breeding grounds in North Russia and Siberia.

The White-front is probably the easiest of the grey geese to recognize as the white forehead and black bars on the belly show up well, even in flight. It also has a characteristic loud cackle which explains one of its country names – the Laughing Goose. At the peak in January and February its numbers may build up to 5000 or more. Experts may spot an occasional Lesser White-front in the flock, distinguished not only by its smaller size but by the larger area of white above the pink bill and a distinctive yellow eye ring. All species of geese on the British list have been recorded on the Dumbles but in much smaller numbers than the White-fronts.

Among the geese there are ducks of many species. There may be as many as 1000 Mallard with a few hundred each of other surface-feeding ducks such as Pintail, Shoveler and Gadwall in the wet fields. On the riverside mud and on the 'scrapes' excavated by the Trust are Teal and Widgeon, which occur in their thousands. Shelduck are present all the year round, conspicuous by their large size, white, black and chestnut plumage and bright crimson bills. Huge flocks of Pochard and the black and white Tufted Duck may also be seen on the water. At low tide, the mud and sand provide a good feeding ground for about twenty species of wader. Among the Lapwings, Ringed Plovers, Redshanks, Curlews, Bar-tailed Godwits, Dunlins and others there are occasional vagrant waders from North America. Splendid views are to be had of this great concourse of birds from spacious hides and from the two tall observation towers.

Not everyone who visits Slimbridge realizes that the reserve stands near to Berkeley Castle, a rugged Norman fortress which has been in the continuous possession of the Berkeley family for 800 years. Over the centuries it has been adapted as a private residence, but some of the kitchens, cellars and dungeons are still exactly as they were when King Edward II was murdered here. Berkeley Castle with all its history well repays a visit.

It is partly thanks to protection provided by the Earls of Berkeley down the centuries that even wary wild birds such as the White-fronted Geese have come to look on the Dumbles as the most important of their winter homes in Britain. Sir Peter Scott could have found no better site than Slimbridge for the Wildfowl Trust and no more sympathetic landlord than the Berkeley family.

Sometimes the sudden appearance of a Peregrine, Merlin or Sparrowhawk will produce a splendid spectacle. In a trice, all is panic: honking groups of geese lift off heavily, but not without grace; ducks and waders become rapidly airborne; and the varied flocks criss-cross each other in a wonderful display of aerial agility above the flat meadow-land of the River Severn.

Another of the Trust's showpieces is Swan Lake. Bewick's Swans, unlike the White-fronted Geese, had not traditionally wintered on the Severn Estuary. They were formerly a comparative rarity in this country, mostly wintering further west in Ireland or further east on the Ouse Washes; but their adaptability and opportunism in recognizing the Trust's sanctuary brought them to Slimbridge in increasing numbers. They are the smallest of the three European wild swans and are named in honour of the celebrated 18th-century ornithologist and engraver Thomas Bewick. The very first one at Slimbridge was decoyed down on 3 November 1948 by a tame bird in the collection – a North American Whistling Swan. In that same year, a wild Bewick's Swan injured in Holland was presented to the Trust and became the first Bewick's to breed in captivity. Known as Mrs Noah, she is still in the collection area and now aged at least thirty-five! Gradually, over the years the numbers have built up: more and more wild Bewick's land here gratefully after the 2500-mile flight from their breeding grounds on the Yamal Peninsula in Siberia. On Slimbridge's Swan Lake, in front of Sir Peter's studio window, the birds find sanctuary and food: a wheelbarrow full of wheat is scattered by a warden twice a day. A flock of 600 or more, together with Mute Swans, Canada and Greylag Geese, Shovelers, Pintails, Pochard and Tufted Duck, can be seen resting and feeding on the lake on most days in winter.

Bewick's stay paired for life and return each year with their offspring from the Arctic in close-knit families. Slimbridge scientists have proved this by capturing some of the birds and fixing around their legs coloured plastic rings marked clearly with numbers. These can then be identified with the help of binoculars at a range of up to 300 yards. It has also been discovered that each Bewick's has an individual pattern of black and yellow on its bill, so that each bird can be identified as surely as fingerprints distinguish humans.

Extensive studies of the birds have been made; they have even been given names and each one has its own dossier. Nothing is left to chance at Slimbridge and in severe frost the water is kept from icing over by the action of submerged air bubblers. At dusk it is a sight of breath-taking beauty when the lake is floodlit and the great gathering of white birds shines with an unearthly brilliance. From early November to the end of February this fine spectacle can be enjoyed from the visitors' hide on the edge of Swan Lake in the big Rushy Pen enclosure or from the indoor Members' Swan Observatory.

Heading the list of attractions among the exotic species in a series of pens and enclosures are the flamingoes. Flocks of all six kinds in the world are kept here and delight visitors with their bizarre appearance and startling shades of crimson and pink. Four species now breed here regularly, which happens nowhere else. Heated houses are provided for them during severe winter weather.

In the general collection there is an almost bewildering diversity of birds assembled from all over the world. Several of the species were until recently in danger of extinction and owe their very survival to the security given at Slimbridge, where in many cases the scientific study of their needs has induced them to breed. This is a most important aspect of the Wildfowl Trust's work.

One of the biggest successes has been with the Hawaiian Goose or Ne-ne, as the native islanders call it because of its soft call. Walking among groups of these friendly little black, grey and brown geese at Slimbridge, it is hard to realize that by the late 1950s there were only thirty-five remaining in the world. The volcanic slopes of Hawaii Island were their last breeding ground. They had been brought to the edge of extinction by overhunting and were also easy prey for dogs, pigs and mongooses. From a small stock kept in captivity by a Hawaiian rancher, Mr Harold Shipman, two females and a male were brought to Slimbridge and eventually bred successfully. By 1962 the stock had become sufficiently large to allow thirty to be taken to Maui in the Hawaiian group of islands and released into the wild. Soon Slimbridge was able to supply Ne-nes to wildfowl research centres throughout the world. As a result, there are now more than 100 on Maui and at least 750 on the neighbouring 'big island' of Hawaii.

Today, the future for this friendly little goose seems assured.

Access By car: from north off M5 at junction 13, from south at junction 14, on to A38, then through Slimbridge village. Free car park. By rail: to Gloucester or Bristol then by bus to within 10 minutes' walk of Gatehouse; or to Stroud and thence by taxi.
Opening times Open daily, except 24 and 25 December, from 9.30 a.m. to 5 p.m.
Facilities Suitable for all the family. Slimbridge is Europe's best-equipped wildfowl refuge; amenities include a restaurant, exhibition, foyer with viewing facilities, shop, guided or self-guided tours, many hides and observation towers, free wheelchairs for the disabled and a comprehensive range of literature. There is also a picnic area. The Wildfowl Trust's education service caters for school and other educational visits led by the Trust's teaching staff.
Warden c/o Wildfowl Trust, Slimbridge, Gloucester GL2 7BT.

CHAPTER FIVE

The Gwenffrwd and Dinas Reserve, Dyfed
RSPB

The reserve of more than 1300 acres is set in the glorious green hill-country of mid-Wales. Apart from the scenic beauty, this is the place to see birds of the woodland and riverside with the chance that a large raptor might well be soaring overhead.

The Gwenffrwd lies 10 miles north of Llandovery and is approached through the little village of Rhandirmwyn in the valley of the Towy. Suddenly, all around there are steep slopes hung with oakwoods; outcrops of grey rock occur among the trees and bracken. Streams show like white threads as they tumble down gullies overhung with alder, ash and birch.

In spring, among the oaks, there is a host of small resident birds with many titmice and the more elusive Nuthatches and Treecreepers. Great Spotted and Green Woodpeckers will certainly be heard if not seen.

There are two colourful little migrants for whom Gwenffrwd has especial importance – the Redstart and the Pied Flycatcher. Both are summer visitors from tropical Africa and both require holes for nesting. Competition for their favourite sites in the decaying branches of trees is keen and so the RSPB has provided numerous

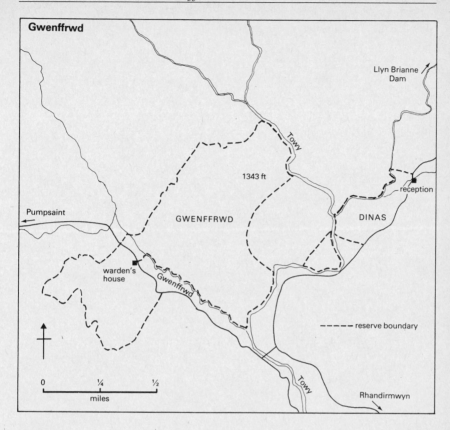

nesting boxes for them. These they have taken to gratefully; in years when caterpillars are plentiful on the oaks as many as 900 Pied Flycatcher fledglings have been reared at Gwenffrwd. The males look distinctly natty in their spring finery of black with a white forehead, white underneath and bars on their wings. They are retiring birds with a preference for the upper branches, so a sharp look-out is necessary. The fiery tails of the Redstarts are much easier to see as the birds constantly quiver their tails in courtship.

Here too among the oaks and birches can be heard the gentle song of the Wood Warbler. A few pairs of Woodcock breed on the reserve but the chances of seeing one of these secretive birds is not great, except on a late spring or summer evening when the males make their roding flights. Buzzards sail overhead on broad wings; Ravens tumble and roll in the air, especially in their aerobatic spring

37

displays. Both species are common at Gwenffrwd. Sparrowhawks are not uncommon and may be seen dashing along the hedgerows in flickering flight.

On the small, fast-running streams there is a good chance of seeing a Dipper. Each pair here needs about a mile stretch of water for its territory. The nests are usually placed among the roots and ferns of steep-sided banks or sometimes even behind a small waterfall, so that the birds have to fly through a curtain of spray to reach their eggs or young. The Dipper is a plump, Wren-shaped bird with dark brown plumage and a conspicuous white breast and one can often be seen in mid-stream, perched on a stone, bowing and curtseying in constant movement. It can also walk upstream under water for about half a minute in search of caddis fly larvae, freshwater shrimps or snails.

Another common breeding bird here is the Grey Wagtail. Like the Dipper, the bird is a true water-sprite. At any moment it may dart upward to snatch a fly or suddenly flicker across the stream, head and neck dipping, and with its elegant 4-inch-long tail in perpetual movement. Common Sandpipers breed in the banks of the Towy and add their shrill piping to the spring chorus. There are usually about fifty pairs of Sand Martins; Herons and Kingfishers are also frequently seen. The scattered farms and outbuildings encourage a host of the commoner birds and there are flocks of more than 100 Chaffinches during the winter months.

One bird above all is associated with Gwenffrwd and it was the main reason for the RSPB setting up the reserve in 1967. The Red Kite, once a common scavenger in the streets of Tudor London, had by the turn of the century been reduced through persecution to as few as three pairs in the whole of Britain. All were in this area of the Upper Towy valley – their last refuge. Local bird protectionists, greatly helped by the RSPB, have now raised their numbers to between twenty and thirty pairs, but they are widely dispersed over the hills of mid-Wales. There is still serious concern that Red Kites and, elsewhere, Golden Eagles, are being killed by illegal poisoning. It is hoped that the Government will finally be persuaded by the RSPB to take firmer action to prevent this deadly and senseless practice.

Nevertheless, with luck, there is still a chance of seeing a Red Kite soaring high in full sunshine or drifting over the oakwoods on angled wings, the unmistakable forked tail tilting with the currents. The pale cream head, bent down to scan the ground, contrasts with the red-brown of back and wings. Owing to the centuries of persecution, Kites have now become shy birds, which makes it all the more important not to stray from paths in the breeding season.

The Dinas is slightly apart from the main Gwenffrwd reserve and close to its eastern boundary. It is an isolated wooded hill at the junction of the rivers Towy and Doethie. If only a short time is available, a walk round the nature trail, which stretches $1\frac{1}{2}$ miles at the base of the hill, will give excellent views of a great variety of birds especially in the breeding season.

In addition to the birds, there are numerous Foxes, which use dens beneath the rock, and Badgers are present in smaller numbers; Rabbits are widespread in small colonies.

Access Turn off the A40 at Llandovery; 10 miles north is the village of Rhandirmwyn. Continue and take the Pumpsaint Road to reach the warden's house.

Opening times Mid-April to end of August on Mondays, Wednesdays and Saturdays only. Report outside the warden's house between 10 a.m. and 2 p.m. The nature trail at Dinas is open throughout the year. Suitable for all the family.

Warden 'Troedrhiwgelynen', Gwenffrwd Reserve, Llandovery, Dyfed.

CHAPTER SIX

The Islands of South West Wales

There are few more beautiful and spectacular stretches of coast in Britain than the 168 miles of Pembrokeshire, which became a National Park in 1952. Pembrokeshire itself now forms part of the larger Welsh county of Dyfed.

In particular, the cliff-top walks of the Dale Peninsula at the entrance to Milford Haven are unrivalled for loveliness and interest. From the red sandstone cliffs strewn with wild flowers there are breathtaking glimpses of rocky coves and wide sandy bays; offshore lie those two islands with the Norse-sounding names, Skomer and Skokholm, and their great colonies of seabirds.

It is because of its millions of seabirds that the British Isles is of such especial importance in the European birdworld. Situated on the western edge of a great land mass, the long indented shore-line, includes many small islands difficult of access, enabling twenty-four species of seabird to breed. The birds are also helped by the warm water of the Gulf Stream that provides a plentiful food supply of small fish close inshore. The best time to see the breeding colonies is from early May to late July.

Surveys show, surprisingly, that our seabird populations are increasing, with the possible exception of the auk family of Puffins, Razorbills and Guillemots and some of the terns. The auks continue to decline mainly because they spend most of their time on the sea's surface and dive for fish, so they frequently become fouled by oil. Another less obvious threat comes from the large ocean-going fishing trawlers fitted with sophisticated radar and sonic equipment. Their nylon nets are almost invisible and, on occasions, have been known to pull up as many diving birds as fish. In some areas, auk numbers have declined owing to shortage of food due to over-fishing.

The other threatened seabirds are those that nest on the foreshore; Little Terns, in particular, often lose their breeding sites through industrialization or perhaps unwitting disturbance by holidaymakers.

The remaining species manage to thrive: some, such as Fulmars and gulls, finding an abundant food supply from the fish offal discarded in harbours and at sea. Gulls also find that rubbish dumps provide even richer pickings. But perhaps the biggest factor in helping seabirds to increase their numbers is that they are no longer shot from boats for sport, as was the case in the 19th century. Neither are they, their young or their eggs, normally, taken for food.

In addition, conservation bodies in Britain, with the RSPB in the forefront, are constantly campaigning for more effective laws to control and reduce the pollution of the oceans. They also seek to help threatened species by acquiring their breeding sites as reserves. This allows the public to see the birds, wherever practicable; in this way new members are gained, and fresh support.

These islands of southwest Wales provide some of the finest bird-watching spectacles in Europe, with tens of thousands of seabirds wheeling and gliding around the close-packed cliff-face colonies.

Although there is no right of public access, there are daily boat trips to or around the main bird islands of Skomer, Skokholm and Ramsey, when weather allows. Grassholm, with its Gannets, lies 10 miles out in the Atlantic and, by special arrangement, may be sailed around in good weather.

Pembrokeshire National Park Guide from:
West Wales Naturalists' Trust, 20A High Street, Haverfordwest, Dyfed.

Dale Fort Field Centre
Field Studies Council

For the able-bodied, who also have some knowledge of small boats, the ideal way to gain access to the islands is to take one of the courses for adult students organized by the Field Studies Council. The Atlantic Islands course lasts a week and is conducted from Dale Fort, poised 100 feet above the sea at the entrance to Milford Haven. The fort buildings were erected in the middle of the last century but have now been converted and modernized to accommodate large numbers of adult students in reasonable comfort.

A former lifeboat is used to take parties of twelve on invigorating and sometimes spray-soaked trips to the islands from April to September. There are several other Natural History courses held at the Fort from March to November. It is advisable to apply well in advance.

Director: Dale Fort Field Centre, Haverfordwest, Dyfed SA62 3RD.

Skomer Island National Nature Reserve
Nature Conservancy Council, West Wales Naturalists' Trust

Of the five main islands, Skomer is the largest and provides the most varied interest. It lies off the southern end of St Bride's Bay: a 200-foot-high plateau covering 720 acres and formed of grey volcanic basalt 400 million years old. Iron Age man was almost certainly here judging by evidence of field systems, huts and enclosures. The Norsemen gave it the name Skalmey, which by the 18th century had become Skomer.

For centuries the principal food crop was Rabbits, which were introduced to the island in the 14th century; the seabirds were also harvested for food. A stone farmhouse was built in the early 18th century, but this is now a complete ruin, except for a small section used as basic accommodation for members of the West Wales Naturalists' Trust. There stands the island's only tree – a black poplar in a sheltered yard. In the 19th century there was extensive

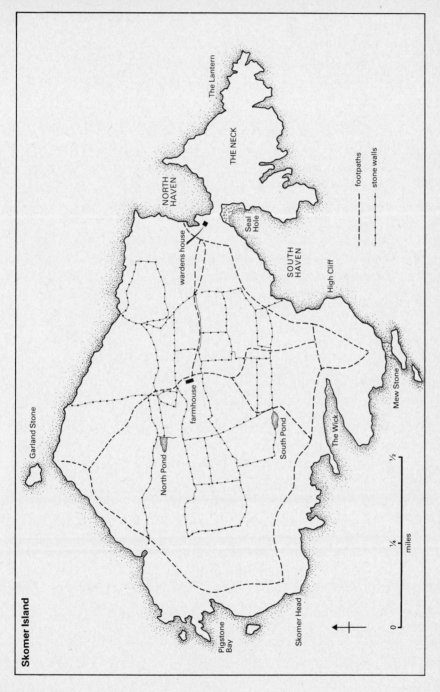

Skomer Island

The Lantern

THE NECK

NORTH HAVEN

Seal Hole

wardens house

SOUTH HAVEN

High Cliff

Garland Stone

farmhouse

North Pond

South Pond

The Wick

Mew Stone

Pigstone Bay

Skomer Head

footpaths

stone walls

½   ¼   0
miles

farming and crops were sent to the mainland. Finally, in 1959 the island was acquired by the Nature Conservancy and the warden's bungalow was built overlooking North Haven. This is the rocky landing place after the twenty-minute boat trip from Martin's Haven or the longer one from Dale. There is then a steep climb to negotiate before following a nature trail extending around the island – a circuit of 4 miles. It is inadvisable to stray from the paths as the island is honeycombed with holes in which the Puffins and Manx Shearwaters nest; damage might be caused unwittingly to the nesting burrows, and personal injury might well result.

In all, there are thirty-seven species of bird breeding on Skomer, but for many people the main attraction will be those melancholy-looking clowns with the gaudy noses and permanently surprised expressions – the Puffins. They may well be seen within a few minutes of the clamber up from the boat. They land abruptly and stand very upright as though arriving for a high-level, dress-suited conference: glistening white fronts, glossy black backs and those incredible scarlet, yellow and blue-grey bills.

Sometimes a Sea Parrot, to give him one of his many common names, may be seen looking important with six or more small fish dangling crosswise from his triangular beak. Having shown his catch, he soon darts down into a burrow to feed the single chick. There are estimated to be 10,000 pairs of Puffins nesting on Skomer: it is now a fairly stable population, but represents a sharp decline over the past thirty years from a peak of 50,000 pairs.

Those other members of the auk family, Guillemots and Razorbills, are best seen across an awe-inspiring inlet known as the Wick. The sheer 200-foot cliff-face of dark, volcanic rock is in places yellow-green with lichens and streaked white with droppings. Lined up along the narrowest ledges opposite will be some 1500 pairs of Guillemots; the noise is indescribable. Chocolate-brown and white with slender, pointed bills, they stand shoulder to shoulder. The birds use no nesting material: the single egg is laid on the bare rock; being pear-shaped it is less likely to roll off. The brood-patch is low on the body, so the egg is held on the feet and pressed against the warm flesh until it hatches.

The Razorbills are black and white with broad, compressed bills like old-fashioned, cut-throat razors. These birds prefer to brood their egg on the slightly broader ledges below an overhang or in crevices; their numbers here are roughly equal to the Guillemots.

Lower down the cliff-face on the narrowest of ledges are the nesting sites of several hundred pairs of Kittiwakes. The air is full of the constant cries from which this small, dark-eyed, dove-like gull gets its name. Other larger members of the gull family circle round piratically, ever ready to seize an unsuspecting chick. Another stockily-built bird glides past on stiff wings exploiting every up-current along the cliff-face. The large, dark eyes and tube nostrils are those of the Fulmar; and they may also be seen nesting on the high crevice at the eastern end of the cliff.

At sea-level, Shags and Cormorants dive for Sprats, Sand-eels and the young of larger fish. The cliff-top path is a splendid vantage-point from which to view this vast, mixed city of seabirds opposite and walking here causes them no disturbance.

Leaving the Wick, the path passes through a profusion of wild flowers: 200 species grow on the island. The soft soil is enriched with centuries of droppings from countless birds and Rabbits. There are also several excellent springs with surrounding areas of wetland. Great drifts of bluebells cover the ground, to be followed in turn by tall fronds of bracken. On the slopes by Skomer Head there are luxurious-looking cushions of pink thrift, interspersed with carpets of white sea campion.

The top of the island belongs to the gulls, which have their close-packed nests among the bluebells and bracken. White necks crane up against the sea of blue as they keep a sharp eye on anyone passing along the path. There are some 5000 pairs of Lesser Black-backed, with their darkish-grey wings and yellow legs, distinguishing them from the silvery-grey backs and flesh-coloured legs of the Herring Gulls, which they outnumber here two to one. Those ferocious predators the Great Black-backed are in very much smaller numbers.

The incessant piping of Oystercatchers and the plaintive cries of Lapwings and Curlews are a delight. In addition, there are five pairs each of Buzzards, Ravens and that daytime hunter, the Short-eared Owl, so there is no lack of variety. It is especially good also to see Wheatears and Stonechats, as they have now become scarce on the mainland; the Wren population is as high as thirty pairs. Jackdaws are numerous, which may partly explain why that most graceful of the crow family, the red-billed and red-legged Chough, no longer breeds on the island, although often seen.

Unfortunately, the most fascinating of all the breeding birds on Skomer, and certainly the most numerous – there are 100,000 pairs – can usually only be seen on land after dark and by the light of a torch: Manx Shearwaters are so called because they used to breed on the Isle of Man in great numbers.

In April, the female lays her single white egg in a shallow burrow on turf slopes near the cliff top. She then flies off, sometimes more than 600 miles to the southern part of the Bay of Biscay, to build up her strength again on Sardines. Meantime, her mate sits on the egg below ground and starves, until her return about six days later. For fifty days the incubation lasts with the parents alternating in almost weekly shifts. The reason for this underground existence is to avoid being snapped up by predatory gulls: Shearwaters are easy prey on land; their webbed feet are set far back on their bodies. The birds are highly specialized for living in the air or on the sea: ashore, they are only able to move with an ungainly shuffle, like very drunken sailors. On dark moonless nights, an unearthly chorus of cries wells up all over the island as the home-coming birds call to their mates in the burrows. Eerie, muffled replies can then be heard coming from below ground.

Manx Shearwaters are black on the upperparts and white underneath. By torchlight the white breasts of the birds seem illuminated, as they crouch in the tussocky grass on their shift-changing routines. To spend a night on Skomer among the 100,000 pairs of Shearwaters is a never-to-be-forgotten experience.

Also under cover of darkness, little Storm Petrels, like plump House Martins with their sooty plumage and white rumps, return on long-winged flight to their tiny holes or crevices in the rocks. So difficult are they to see and locate that their numbers are unknown. They too make strange crooning noises: so, truly, at night, in Shakespeare's words, 'the isle is full of noises'.

There are only five species of mammal on the island excluding bats; one is unique – the Skomer Vole. This is a larger and tamer version of the Bank Vole on the mainland. It is of considerable scientific interest and may eventually be designated a separate species.

The Rabbit abounds and presents a serious over-grazing problem. It is nevertheless of great ecological importance providing food for birds of prey and burrows for seabirds. There is a complete absence of Foxes, Stoats and Weasels; Lizards and Slow Worms are present but no Adders or Grass Snakes. Grey Seals are seen all the year round and particularly during the autumn breeding season when they haul out on the rocks at the Garland Stone to the north of the island.

Access By boat from Martin's Haven (car park) near Marloes, reached on B4327 from Haverfordwest; the boats run daily (departing between 10.30 a.m. and 12.30 p.m. and returning between 3.30 and 4.30 p.m.) and the trip takes about 20 minutes. There is a small landing fee in addition to the boat charges.
Opening times 10.30 a.m. to 4.30 p.m.
Facilities For the able bodied. Warm clothing and waterproofs advisable. Self-guided nature trails of 2 to 4 miles; illustrated booklet available.
Accommodation Short-period accommodation for amateur or professional naturalists, by arrangement with the warden well in advance.
Warden Skomer Island NNR, West Wales Naturalists' Trust, 4 Victoria Place, Haverfordwest, Dyfed.

Skokholm Nature Reserve
West Wales Naturalists' Trust

Skokholm lies 2 miles south of Skomer across the treacherous Broad Sound. It is 1 mile long, ½ mile wide and covers 240 acres, which makes it one-third the size of its neighbour. Apart from this, the main difference between the islands is that Skokholm's cliffs are of Old Red Sandstone, not volcanic rock, and look warm and weathered.

A narrow cleft in the rocks forms a tiny harbour on the south side. This is presided over by a female figurehead mounted half-way up the cliff and dating back to the wreck there of an old wooden schooner, *Alice Williams*, in 1928. A steep track leads up to a whitewashed 18th-century farmhouse, where volunteer wardens can stay for a week or more on Natural History courses.

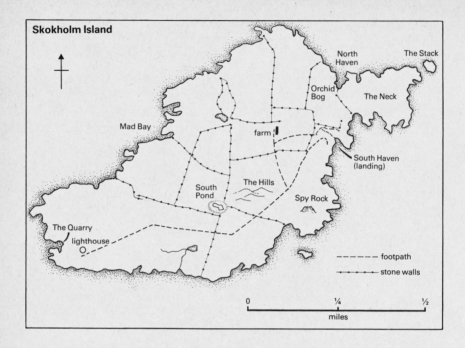

The island will always be associated with the writer and naturalist Ronald Lockley, who farmed the island from 1927 until the outbreak of war in 1939. He built here Britain's first large Heligoland bird trap, and through his ringing activities discovered that British-bred shearwaters spend the winter off the northeast coast of South America. The Skokholm observatory started in 1933 and became the forerunner of a chain of British bird observatories which flourished in the 1950s.

The number of species breeding here is almost the same as on Skomer – thirty-six as against thirty-seven – but there are also many migrants, mostly small song-birds, including some first sightings and recordings for Wales and occasionally for Britain. These visitors are often to be found in spring and autumn near the farmhouse, where they find vegetation and shelter. As on Skomer, the flat top of the island belongs to the Lesser Black-backed Gulls which nest among the colourful drifts of wild flowers and heather. It is advisable to wear a hat, as they often make aggressive swoops at anyone

48

venturing along the paths through their colonies and frequently register a hit.

Access Boat trips around the island from Dale or Martin's Haven near Marloes. Landings, in official groups only, to be arranged in advance with the West Wales Naturalists' Trust, 4 Victoria Place, Haverfordwest, Dyfed.
Facilities For the able bodied. Warm clothing and waterproofs advisable. Trail and hides.
Accommodation Full-board accommodation for members on courses.
Warden Skokholm Bird Observatory, 7 Market Street, Haverfordwest, Dyfed.

Grassholm Nature Reserve RSPB/ West Wales Naturalists' Trust

Grassholm lies 10 miles out in the Atlantic: next stop – America. It is of the same volcanic rock as Skomer and the site of the largest gannetry in England and Wales. The 22-acre uninhabited island is isolated at a turbulent meeting place of tide races and swift currents. Only in the best of weather can this sanctuary of the Gannet, or Solan Goose, be approached; even the Dale lifeboat must proceed with utmost caution. From afar, the northwestern heights of the island appear white, as though capped with snow, so great is the concentration of birds. A little nearer, and there is swirling movement to be seen like clouds of white smoke; then soon, all around and above the boat there are thousands of the great cigar-shaped birds scything the air with white wings tipped with black and measuring fully 6 feet across.

There is no harbour, but, in perfect weather conditions, a landing can be made direct on to the slippery rocks by means of a rubber dinghy launched from the main craft. Meantime, seals, hauled out on the rocks, gaze curiously at the intrusion. A steep climb follows up to the northwest slopes and, suddenly, there is the Gannet high-rise fortress – a 2-acre carpet of white.

It is a strange sensation to be alone with 17,500 pairs of these gaunt, imperious-looking birds. A gannetry is a highly organized club. Young birds have to learn from example and hard experience.

They will probably not breed until they are six to ten years old and meantime are only allowed to nest on the outer edges of the colony. There, they soon discover that a wandering chick or an unguarded egg will quickly be gobbled up by the ever-waiting gulls.

The chicks at first are lead-grey in colour; they soon grow a covering of white down, and dark feathers follow. First-year birds are dark with speckled markings and gradually become whiter with successive moults until the gleaming white of adulthood is attained at four years old.

The nests are mostly of seaweed and flotsam of all kinds and piled sometimes 18 to 24 inches high. They are packed close together but just out of range of a neighbour's bayonet-like bill. The chicks are fed on regurgitated fish; their heads disappear into the parent's gullet to swallow the semi-digested meal. The smell of a Gannet colony is unforgettable: a noisome stench of seaweed, decayed fish and caked white droppings. There is constant coming and going. They land heavily with wings, tail and broad feet spread. Should a bird overshoot, it will have to run a gauntlet of stabs and blows until it gains its own nesting mound.

When taking off, a Gannet stands erect, facing into the wind, with bill pointing skyward, as though signalling his departure. Above and all around the island these great white birds with pointed tails circle and plane. They often plunge-dive from heights of 30 feet or more for mackerel and other fish lying in shoals near the surface. Sometimes they hit the water with considerable impact. The shock is withstood thanks to the especially adapted skull and the air sacs under the skin. The nostrils too are protected and concealed inside the unique steel-blue bill.

It is good to know that the world population of the Northern Gannet now approaches 200,000 pairs. Their success is largely due to the fact that the breeding colonies are at last protected and the birds are scarcely ever cropped for food.

In addition to Gannets and seals, Grassholm has Greater Black-backed and Herring Gulls, Guillemots, Razorbills, Kittiwakes and Shags.

Enquiries should be made to West Wales Naturalists' Trust, 4 Victoria Place, Haverfordwest, Dyfed.

Ramsey Island Nature Reserve
Private

Ramsey lies less than a mile offshore from the small cathedral city of St David's at the northern end of St Bride's Bay. Not a great distance, but in between are the difficult waters of Ramsey Sound with a perilous ridge of rocks, known as The Bitches, where the tidal race swirls and froths.

The 600-acre island has seen much history and for centuries belonged to the Bishops of St David's. It has links with the first Celtic missionaries to Britain and one of them, St Dyfanog, ended his days on Ramsey about AD 186.

It is a scenically beautiful island but the bird life is rather limited. This is due to Rats, which prevent the breeding of burrow-nesting birds. On the other hand, there are splendid views of the cliff-nesting seabirds, which are best seen from a boat.

Close to the farmhouse, above the landing-stage, there is a good chance of seeing a few Choughs. These elegant members of the crow family are now rare and mainly confined to the western coasts of Britain and Ireland. It is a delight to watch their acrobatic flying displays and then to admire them more closely, as they probe the turf with their curved bills of sealing-wax red.

This is also the best island for seeing the Grey Atlantic Seals, especially in the autumn when they have their pups. In 1978 the then owner (Robin Pratt) introduced a herd of Red Deer as an experimental replacement for the sheep and cattle, which until the 1930s had controlled the vegetation on Ramsey.

Ramsey is a privately owned island (nature reserve). It has recently changed hands. It is assumed that visits are still allowed, daily during July and August, and out of season by prior arrangement with the owner. Trips around the island are also possible. Boats from St Justinians, 1½ miles west of St David's. There is a car park near embarkation point. Dogs are not allowed on the island, and camping and smoking are discouraged. Owner: (John Freeman) Ramsey Island Nature Reserve, St David's, Haverfordwest, Dyfed.

Caldy Island
Private

For those averse to small open boats, slippery rocks and steep climbs, Caldy is by far the easiest of the islands to visit. It lies off the south coast of Pembrokeshire close to the holiday resort of Tenby. Cistercian monks own and farm the island, but they welcome visitors and in high summer receive as many as 2000 a day.

Only $1\frac{1}{2}$ miles long and $\frac{2}{3}$ mile wide, it is more sheltered than the other islands and, as it has trees and shrubs, including pines and fuchsias, more song-birds are able to breed. The coastline is varied, with sandy bays and limestone rocks in the north and Old Red Sandstone in the south. There are also high cliffs for breeding seabirds.

Adjoining Caldy to the west is St Margaret's Island with the biggest colony of Cormorants in Wales.

There are frequent passenger boats to the island from Tenby. Landing is permitted Monday to Friday from Whitsun until the end of September. Boat trips round the island are available on Saturdays and Sundays, also from Tenby.

CHAPTER SEVEN

Bardsey Nature Reserve, Gwynedd
Bardsey Trust

Of all the Welsh islands there is none more isolated and yet more cherished since ancient times than Bardsey. In Welsh, its name Ynys Enlli means the Island in the Tiderace, and nothing could be more apt than that. Bardsey lies 2 miles off the southwestern tip of the Lleyn Peninsula, which juts out into the Irish Sea to form the northern arm of Cardigan Bay. The nearest harbour of any size is Pwllheli, 19 miles distant; an open fishing boat takes three hours to make the crossing. With a sea whipped up by savage westerly gales it may be impossible to cross from the mainland and the island can then be cut off for a week or more.

There are several traces of human occupation from the Stone Age. Flakes of flint and chippings of rock have been found near one of the farmhouses named Carreg Fawr. The six listed ancient monuments include a round barrow on Mynydd Enlli that some think dates from the Bronze Age, and there are also hut circles. Three others are relatively modern: a stone slab carved with a cross, now built into the wall of Hen-dy farm, is ascribed to the period of the 7th to 9th centuries; another carved stone shows the lower half of a small figure wearing a pleated skirt or kilt and dates from the 10th or 11th century; and then in the 23-foot-high ruins of the tower of the Augustinian Abbey of St Mary there are lancet windows of the 13th century. But Bardsey was evidently of great importance as a religious centre long before that.

It was perhaps because of its isolation that the early Celtic saints chose to be buried at this extreme westerly point, as near as possible to the setting sun; here also there was security from grave robbers and Wolves. For this reason, Bardsey was once known as the Island of Bones: 20,000 saints, confessors and martyrs are thought to have been buried here, and in the Middle Ages it was considered that three pilgrimages to the island were the equivalent of one to Rome. This assessment probably took into account the perils of crossing the turbulent waters of Bardsey Sound. At the church of Llanaber, in the little port of Barmouth on the mainland, there was even a holding-place where the corpses used to be kept to await favourable weather.

The monks were able to enjoy the security and isolation of their island for a thousand years and remained members of the Culdees, the Irish branch of the Celtic Church, until nearly the end of the 12th century. Finally, their world was shattered by the dissolution of the monasteries under Henry VIII.

Thereafter, it was inhabited by only a few sheepfarmers and fishermen and became at one time a stronghold for pirates. Bardsey also had a king who was crowned by one of the Barons Newborough, who were the owners of the island from the 16th century. The last king appeared at the Pwllheli National Eisteddfod in 1924, when David Lloyd George referred to him as 'one of the Welsh from overseas'.

This sense of isolation is increased by the fact that Bardsey presents its back to the world. Seen from the mainland, it appears little more than a hump of rock. The 550-foot cliffs of the eastern edge hide a patchwork of small banked meadows sloping away to the sea. Bardsey covers 450 acres and is only $1\frac{3}{4}$ miles long and $\frac{3}{4}$ mile across at its widest point and yet it holds a considerable variety of scene.

To the south, a narrow spray-washed neck of land leads to a small, gorse-studded area dominated at the centre by the square red and white tower of the lighthouse. From here, the island's one road

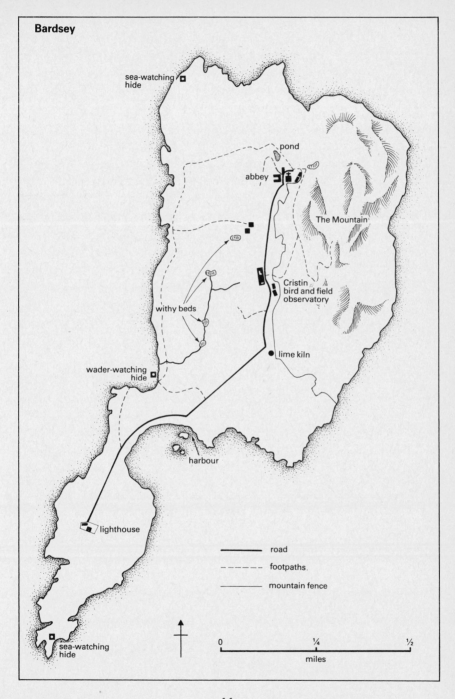

Bardsey

sea-watching hide

pond

abbey

The Mountain

withy beds

Cristin bird and field observatory

lime kiln

wader-watching hide

harbour

lighthouse

sea-watching hide

road

footpaths

mountain fence

0   ¼   ½
miles

leads northward, passing a sheltered inlet, the Cafn, which is the landing place; it then carries on and finally peters out among the abbey ruins. Beside the road are ten sturdy, stone farmhouses, some of which are being renovated by the Trust for the accommodation of visitors and staff. One of these, named Cristin, sheltering behind buttressed walls, houses the Bird and Field Observatory, set up in 1953. It can be arranged to stay a week or longer here and everyone is welcome, whether a professional ornithologist or just a beginner in search of peace.

At Cristin it is possible to join in counts and observations of breeding and migrant birds carried out by the permanent staff. In all, forty-one species have been recorded over the years as nesting, though not all of them regularly. The most memorable experience may well be the catching and ringing of Manx Shearwaters, those long, narrow-winged birds of the ocean.

On moonless nights, so as to be unseen by predators, the shearwaters fly in to their nesting burrows and fill the air with weird sounds – a ghostly chorus; some visitors might think they were hearing the cries of troubled saints. As these strange birds can only be seen by torchlight, an accurate count is impossible, but their numbers on Bardsey have been put at around 4000 breeding pairs.

Since the ringing of Manx Shearwater chicks began in 1953 some 10,000 have been marked. Many are recaptured years later but several have been notified as killed abroad; the most distant was a report from Santos in Brazil. There was one remarkable case of a chick ringed in 1958 on Skokholm Island to the south being found breeding on Bardsey in 1979, twenty-one years later.

Probably the best-loved birds on the island are those rare and elegant members of the crow family – the Choughs. Red-billed and red-legged, they are a delight to watch in their tumbling butterfly-like flights and seem to have no fear of people. There are about seven pairs nesting in deep crevices of the cliffs, but sometimes flocks of them can be seen playing in the up-currents and their musical cries hang on the air.

A few pairs of their more formidable relatives, the Carrion Crows and Ravens, nest on the island, and sometimes they harry the

Oystercatchers and other shore-birds. Ravens have been seen digging at a Shearwater burrow in daylight. Other seabirds include a few hundred pairs of Razorbills and smaller numbers of Guillemots and Shags. Five pairs of Little Owls, introduced into Britain in the last century, nest on Bardsey and there is a good chance of seeing one, hunting by day. There are also many Rock Pipits, with distinctive grey, outer tail-feathers, among the smaller residents.

Apart from the breeding birds, Bardsey's big attraction in spring or autumn is the possibility of 'falls' of migrants. On overcast, rainy nights when the stars are obscured, small birds such as Willow Warblers may have difficulty in navigating and they sometimes land on the island in thousands. On occasions there are extreme rarities as well: wind-blown strays from the Mediterranean, Eastern Europe, the Arctic or North America. In all, the observatory has recorded more than 250 species of birds.

In addition to weather hazards, birds migrating at night find the Bardsey Lighthouse a deadly attraction. The five 270,000-candle-power beams stab the night sky every fifteen seconds. In bad weather, the birds become confused and, dazzled by the glare, they then crash against the lantern itself or collide with the 99-foot-high tower, the glazing or dome.

The Warden, Peter Roberts, described such a night on 18 August 1977: 'Thousands of Willow Warblers (398 were caught and ringed) and hundreds of Sedge Warblers and Grasshopper Warblers were present. Virtually the whole Observatory was up to watch this spectacular phenomenon with its bewildering array of birds. Bardsey's first Dotterel to be ringed was picked up below the tower, and a remarkable 19 species of wader were seen and heard around the lantern, including Bardsey's first recorded Wood Sandpiper; and small flocks of Little Stints called eerily as they circled the light, and then drifted away, never to be seen by the light of day. 548 birds were ringed during that night, and an already-ringed Storm Petrel was caught. And 149 birds were killed on that night alone.'

To witness one of these occasions from the ground below the lantern is an unforgettable sight. The flocks become a host of tiny moving stars as they are caught in the sweeping beams. Many of the birds perpetually call, as though in distress. On some nights, eighteen species have been identified, if one includes the dead bodies collected at the foot of the tower in the morning.

Trinity House, the RSPB and other naturalists' organizations have for years carried out experiments in an attempt to reduce the casualties. The most successful method now being used is to illuminate the gorse-covered ground below the lighthouse. When this is done on these nights of attraction, many hundreds of birds will just rest peacefully on the grass or take shelter from wind and rain in the floodlit bushes.

In addition to the birds, Bardsey has other attractions: Grey Seals haul out on rocks off the west coast of the island and on warm summer nights their soulful songs blend with the eerie cries of Shearwaters. Connemara ponies and Mountain Sheep peacefully graze. Rabbits are numerous, although their numbers fluctuate with outbreaks of myxomatosis; happily for ground-nesting birds, there are no Foxes or Rats.

Wild flowers grow in profusion: in all nearly 300 species of flowering plants and ferns have been identified. In spring and summer the cliff tops shimmer with sea pinks and sea campion, the damp meadows of the west are bright with yellow flags and marsh marigolds, and the slopes of the little mountain are covered with foxgloves and wild thyme. The withy beds are fed by springs from the rocky mountainside. There are also marsh and spotted orchids and one of the rarities is the autumn lady's tresses. Pellitory-of-the-wall is common on the farmhouse walls and grows among the ruins of the abbey. Of particular interest are the numerous wild-growing herbs introduced centuries ago by the monks to help cure their ailments: among them are wormwood, applemint and elecampane.

There was considerable concern in the mid-1970s when this island of such exceptional importance to wildlife and with its unique heritage came up for sale for the second time within a few years. The Bardsey Bird and Field Observatory Council decided something must be done: an appeal for £200,000 was launched for its purchase and endowment and the money was raised within two years. Donations came from hundreds of concerned individuals and from the World Wildlife Fund, the Nature Conservancy Council, the Countryside Commission and the Bird Observatory itself, which was the fourth largest donor. The Bardsey Trust was formed and the 'island in the tiderace' is now part of Britain's national heritage with its future as a nature reserve assured.

Access By boat from Pwllheli every Saturday, weather permitting. Visitors should be at the Lifeboat House by 8.30 a.m. – cars may be left here during a stay on the island. For short day-trips to the island contact the Trust Officer, Mr David Thomas, Tyddyn Du Farm, Criccieth, Gwynedd. Tel: 076-671 2239.

Opening times From late March to early November.

Bookings To be made well in advance to the Bookings Secretary, 21a Gestridge Road, Kingsteignton, Newton Abbot, Devon. Tel: 0626-68580.

Facilities For the able bodied. Warm clothing and waterproofs advisable. Tuition courses (full board) available – details from the Bookings Secretary.

Accommodation Stays – for one or more weeks – are in Cristin Farmhouse, self-catering. There is a resident warden. The Bardsey Trust has renovated other farmhouses where accommodation is available – apply to the Trust Officer.

CHAPTER EIGHT

The Dee Estuary Reserves, Clwyd, Cheshire and Merseyside

The Wirral Peninsula projects into the Irish Sea like an ageing molar from a deeply receding gum. It separates the wide expanse of the Dee Estuary, flanked by the green hills of north Wales, from the industrial bustle of the Mersey on the English side.

Time has brought it many a change: up to medieval days the huge and nearly rectangular mouth of the Dee stretched back 20 miles to the walled Roman city of Chester, which at that time was the chief port in the northwest. Gradually, over the centuries, extensive silting occurred until by the 18th century the River Mersey with its great port of Liverpool finally took over from the diminishing Dee. Yet even today the estuary still stretches back 12 miles and reaches 5 miles across.

At first glance, it may appear nothing but a flat, wide desolation but for the birdwatcher it is one of the most important places for migrant waders and waterfowl in Britain. It forms a vital link in the west coast chain of feeding areas, the others being Solway, Morecambe Bay and the nearby Ribble.

At low-tide, this vast expanse of sand and mud becomes a rich larder of food for birds. The river washes down humus and minerals from the hills and valleys; the flooding tide adds its salty quota, until the resulting mud teems with Lugworms, Ragworms, shrimps and smaller crustaceans, molluscs and crabs.

The waders, or shore-birds as the Americans call them, have bills of varying length and shape so that each group is able to find its food at different depths. The sensitive, downward-curving probe of the Curlew is the longest and enables it to reach worms 6 inches down. At the other extreme is the short strong levering bill of the Turnstone, ideally suited for feeding along the tide-line, where it searches tirelessly among the pebbles and seaweed for insects and small shellfish.

There is one distinct advantage in watching birds on mudflats – they can be readily seen; but a knowledge of local tides is essential before choosing a vantage point. Charles Kingsley's words about the lone cattle-girl Mary must never be forgotten:

> The western tide crept up along the sand,
> And o'er and o'er the sand,
> And round and round the sand,
> As far as eye could see,
> the rolling mist came down and hid the land:
> and never home came she.

Nevertheless, given a fine, clear day, there can be breath-taking sights as tens of thousands of waders wheel in the air like wind-blown smoke or mass together, a close-knit carpet, at high-tide roosts. There are many viewing places along the three sides of this watery wilderness, from the Red Rocks off Hoylake at the northeast corner down to Burton Marsh in the south and then up the Clwyd coast to the Point of Air. On some days in winter this great estuary of the Dee may hold some 140,000 birds – a tenth of the total number of waders in Britain.

For the most part, their breeding grounds are in the high Arctic from Greenland to eastern Siberia. Some pass the winter at the estuary, others are only seen while on passage to feeding places further south. The biggest concentrations of all occur along the shore on the English side at the top corner, where the estuary meets the sea. West Kirby and the Red Rocks, with the little Hilbre Islands just ½ mile offshore, can provide the most remarkable spectacle of massed birds to be seen anywhere in Britain. As high-tide approaches, the rising waters drive the feeding birds off the mudflats and with a great roar of wings they cascade down on to the rocks and quiet stretches of shoreline. So closely packed are they that some birds are forced to land on the heads and backs of others until they can gradually insinuate themselves into the dense throng. Meantime, the sound stuns the senses until finally they settle, heads tucked beneath wings, a living carpet of grey, to await the turn of the tide; a strange quiet descends.

Most numerous of the waders are the Knot and Dunlin: there may well be flocks of more than 40,000 of both species. Some of the Knot may spend the winter as far south as Australia and New Zealand but many remain. In winter their plumage is a mottled grey with paler underparts. They crowd together more closely than any other wader and in flight move like dense rain-clouds, swirling about the sky in uncanny unison. At rest, the Knot is seen to be of medium size: squat, plump and with a short bill. The summer plumage is in total contrast. Face, throat and underparts are then suffused with russet and this is how they are often seen when on passage from or to their Arctic breeding grounds in autumn and spring respectively. The name Knot was once thought to have derived from King Canute, as the bird certainly defies the waves when feeding along the shoreline, but now it is thought more likely to stem from the alarm cry 'knoot'.

The Dunlin is smaller and the commonest of our waders: there are some to be seen on the estuary throughout the year. A small proportion nest in Britain mainly on upland moors, but the majority occur as winter visitors and passage migrants. In summer plumage they are easily identified by their black bellies.

Other waders for whom the Dee is of international importance are the Godwits (Bar-tailed and Black-tailed), Curlew, Oystercatcher, Sanderling and Redshank. The best time for seeing these great masses of waders at rest, each species grouped together, is about 2 hours before high-tide from late summer to late spring.

As the tide ebbs, it is equally fascinating to watch the great flocks peel away from their roosts and spread out over the glistening expanse of uncovered mud and sand. Small, dumpy Sanderlings, much whiter than others of their size, dart along on twinkling feet to pick up food at the very edge of the water. The slightly bigger Knots and Dunlins mill about in busy flocks; Oystercatchers, outstanding with their orange-red bills and legs and natty black and white plumage, search for cockles and the other molluscs on which only they can feed, yet they continually protest with comical high-pitched pipings. The worm- and shrimp-eating Redshanks flute and yodel, their brown plumage less distinct against the mud. Curlews and Bar-tailed Godwits, stately on their long legs, stand out from the crowd, as they scan the sand for signs of deep-down worms. Lapwings and Grey Plovers also move slowly looking and listening for food on and just below the surface.

Among the great throng will be many other common species and several rarer birds – Little Stints and Curlew Sandpipers from the Arctic, Kentish Plovers, Whimbrels, Spotted Redshanks and Greenshanks from less distant European breeding grounds, and the occasional chance straggler from North America.

Low-tide is also the time to see more of the thousands of wildfowl feeding on the mudflats. From September to March the estuary becomes an especially important staging post for that aristocrat among ducks, the elegant Pintail, with tail streamers fully 8 inches long, a chocolate-coloured head and white breast. In mid-winter there may be as many as 6000 Pintails present; some of these will be on passage from Iceland, north and central Russia and parts of Siberia. The Shelduck, more the size of a goose, with its blackish-green, chestnut and white plumage and gaudy scarlet bill, is also here in large numbers. In autumn there may be about 4000 and some stay to breed. Mallard are common at all times; a few hundred Teal and Wigeon stay during October and November; and at high-tide on the Wirral side of the estuary many Water Rails may be seen when flushed out from their feeding areas in waterside vegetation.

Fish-eating birds – gulls, terns, skuas and some sea ducks – are best seen at either corner of the mouth of the estuary, from Hilbre and Red Rocks on the Wirral corner and from the Point of Air on the Welsh side. Sea ducks including good numbers of Scaup, Goldeneye and Red-breasted Mergansers can be seen in winter. Red-throated Divers and Great Crested Grebes are also often present but other divers and grebes are rare. Common Scoters are few in number but regularly seen; Velvet Scoters, Eiders and Long-tailed Ducks occur occasionally near the mouth of the estuary when there is rough weather at sea.

Although mostly quiet, the estuary is not without several pockets of industry. These are well dispersed, mainly on the Welsh side and at the inland southern extremity. Even this development is not entirely unfavourable to wildlife. Within the vast steelworks at Shotton and the power station at Connah's Quay for instance, areas have been set aside as nature reserves. These are so expertly managed that many birds are able to feed and breed there and they have become popular birdwatching sites.

A big factor in the relentless silting up of the estuary, especially at the southern end, was the introduction of Spartina. This is a cord-grass which binds the sand; silt can then form around its stems. Soon marshes developed and became good grazing for sheep. Other plants of the saltings took hold – glasswort, sea meadow-grass and sea aster. Of the 31,500 acres of the Dee estuary now remaining, 6000 are of well-vegetated saltmarsh, which continues to encroach on the open tidal sands and mud. This has meant a loss of feeding grounds for waders and wildfowl and a corresponding increase in nesting sites for Redshanks, Lapwings, Mallard, Oystercatchers and Snipe. Skylarks, Meadow Pipits and Reed Buntings breed over a wide area and small numbers of Yellow Wagtail also nest.

In some places reed-beds have developed where Sedge, Reed and Grasshopper Warblers breed. Good numbers of Sandwich, Arctic, Common and Little Terns are seen on passage in spring and autumn, while a few of the latter two species breed around the estuary. In the summer they can be seen feeding up to the southern end and along the channel to Connah's Quay. West Kirby beach, Hilbre and the Point of Air are especially favoured in early summer by Little Terns for roosting and offshore feeding.

While wildlife is the paramount attraction of the estuary, there is a wealth of historic interest too. Chester itself was a prosperous city and port in Roman times. After the Romans' withdrawal came the marauding Danes and Saxons. Under the Normans it revived again, and by the 13th century had become the principal port in the northwest, serving Scotland, Ireland, France and Spain. The Dee then began silting up, and by the 15th century the seaborne trade had mostly died. Throughout all its history, Chester has retained its ancient city walls that extend in a 2-mile circuit. There is no finer example in Britain of a fortified, medieval town. It became a Royalist stronghold in the Civil War and from one of the towers Charles I saw his cavaliers go down to defeat at Rowton Heath in 1645. The past seems to live again in Chester. Among all the splendid examples of Tudor and Elizabethan buildings is Bishop Lloyd's House built in 1591. Apart from the walls, perhaps the most memorable feature of the city is The Rows. These are unique and remain much as they must have appeared in the 14th century with a continuous line of shops at street and first-floor levels.

Another place dreaming of the past is the once prosperous fishing village of Parkgate on the south of the Wirral. Its greatest days were in the 18th century, when something like twenty inns were built to handle the passenger traffic to Ireland. A traveller of that time described it as: 'a constant moving picture of ships, sea plants on the beach, seaweed and beautiful shells'. Handel disembarked here after conducting *The Messiah* in Dublin, and John Wesley often passed through on his preaching missions. It also became a favoured holiday resort. The future Lady Hamilton, Nelson's mistress, stayed here, as did Mrs Fitzherbert, consort of the Prince Regent. But, inexorably, the mud and vegetation took over until by 1940 the local fishing boats, or 'nobbies', could no longer use the sandstone quay. Parkgate with all its memories now looks out over nothing but a vast expanse of saltings.

The Hilbre Islands Bird Observatory

At low-tide, the islands are within walking distance of West Kirby near the northwest corner of the Wirral Peninsula. They are perhaps the most famous site of all from which to see the tight-packed masses of waders. Until 1610 Hilbre was shown in maps as a single island

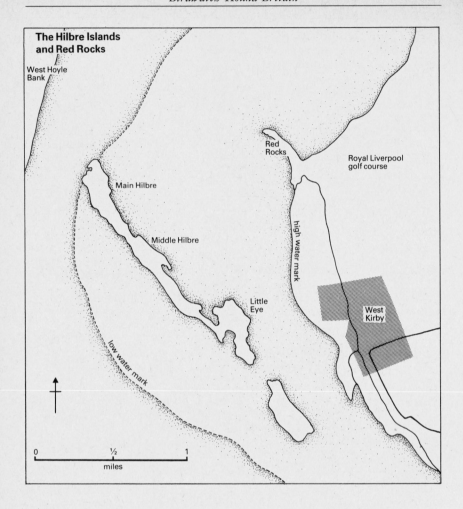

The Hilbre Islands
and Red Rocks

West Hoyle
Bank

Red
Rocks

Royal Liverpool
golf course

Main Hilbre

Middle Hilbre

high water mark

Little
Eye

West
Kirby

low water mark

0   ½   1
miles

about a mile square. Now, after centuries of pounding by the sea, only three islets survive: Main Hilbre, $11\frac{1}{2}$ acres, Middle Hilbre, 3 acres, and the Eye, just $\frac{1}{2}$ acre.

An observatory was set up here in 1957 and has recorded some 230 species. Among several recoveries of birds ringed at Hilbre were a Purple Sandpiper, shot five years later by an Eskimo in Greenland, and a Turnstone, found in Iceland eight years after ringing. Apart from the wealth of birds, a non-breeding herd of Grey Seals, occasionally 200 strong in summer, can be seen hauled out on the Hoyle Bank.

When visiting the islands great care should be taken to obtain local advice about tide times and the route across the sands around the Little Eye. To remain on Hilbre over high-tide, it is necessary to leave the mainland at Dee Lane, West Kirby, 3 hours before high-water. The return can be made about $2\frac{1}{2}$ hours after high-tide. Warm clothing is advisable.

Permits are required for the main island and are obtainable from The Leisure Services Department, Wirral Borough Council, 8 Riversdale Road, West Kirby, Wirral, Merseyside, who manage the reserve.

Hilbre Bird Observatory's annual report can be obtained on the island or from The Director, J. C. Gittins, 17 Deva Road, West Kirby, Merseyside.

The Red Rocks Nature Reserve

The Red Rocks Ringing Station helps manage the reserve in conjunction with the Cheshire Conservation Trust.

Besides being an excellent vantage point for the observation of birds at sea and the mass flighting and roosting of waders, there is also a well-vegetated, brackish marsh; a good variety of birds can therefore be expected. Fieldfares, Redwings, Bramblings and occasionally Snow Buntings pass by, with peak numbers in October. Staying to feed in the cover there may be pipits, warblers and tits. Rare vagrants such as the Melodious and Great Reed Warbler, Richard's Pipit, Wryneck and Bluethroat have been seen and on occasion ringed.

Access to the reserve is by boat from Hoylake or West Kirby. Warm clothing is advisable. Prior application is not required and entry is unrestricted, although visiting is preferred between August and April. For further details contact Mrs J. Milner, Secretary Cheshire Conservation Trust (Wirral Group), 48 Moreton Road, Upton, Wirral, Merseyside, or to Red Rocks Ringing Station, D. Woodward, 3 Tudorville Road, Bebington, Merseyside.

The Gayton Sands Reserve

These 5000 acres of intertidal mudflats and saltings near Parkgate were acquired by the RSPB in 1979. This was an important conservation victory. The Dee Estuary Conservation Group comprises eighteen local and national bodies including the RSPB, the British Trust for Ornithology, the Cheshire Conservation Trust, the Cheshire Community Council, the North Wales Naturalists' Trust, the Wildfowlers' Association of Great Britain and Ireland and the Wildfowl Trust.

Gayton Sands is one of the best sites for watching wildfowl and, at high-tide, the waders. In late autumn, as many as 5000 Shelduck and 6000 Pintail may occur. In winter, concentrations of Water Rails gather in the cord-grass adjoining the sea-wall in the Parkgate area. The large stretches of saltmarsh plants attract good numbers of seed-eating finches and, occasionally, Kestrels or Sparrowhawks prey on them. Merlins, Peregrines, Hen Harriers and Short-eared Owls are regular winter visitors.

There is a viewpoint at Parkgate, near Heswall on the A540, which covers all the western side of the Wirral. Visiting arrangements are yet to be announced by the RSPB. It is dangerous to venture on to the marsh.

Shotton Steelworks Nature Reserve

As the name suggests – another success for conservation. This small wilderness of pools, reed-beds and flowering plants is situated at the foot of the estuary surrounded by a steel and concrete jungle. In 1967 the Merseyside Ringing Group planted scrub to attract breeding birds and migrants. With the help of the British Steel Corporation they then built floating platforms in the steelworks' cooling tanks to provide a safe nesting site for Common Terns. Soon, a colony of 150 pairs became established and won for the Group the Prince of Wales Award for Conservation.

In addition, reserve management has made it possible for Whinchats, Wheatears, Cuckoos and Reed and Sedge Warblers to breed. Black Terns are often seen in summer, and winter visitors include Bearded Tits, Rock and Water Pipits, waders and birds of prey. In all over 200 species have been recorded.

Entry to the reserve is from the works entrance on the A548, west of the junction with the A550. A permit is necessary and application should be made to Personnel Services, British Steel Corporation, Shotton Works, Deeside.

Connah's Quay Nature Reserve

This lies just downstream from Shotton and is another excellent example of a big public industry co-operating with local naturalists. In 1975 the Central Electricity Generating Board and the Deeside Naturalists' Society together developed 90 acres of shore to the north of the power station. A variety of protected habitats for birds resulted: bare tidal mud and saltmarsh, embanked pools of brackish water, where evaporation can be replaced by fresh water brought in by a wind-pump; there are also wader scrapes, reed-beds and scrub. A hide provides excellent views of numerous birds of passage: Spotted Redshank, Greenshank, Green Sandpiper, and Snipe in winter; Wood Sandpipers, Little Stints, Curlew Sandpipers and Ruffs in the migration seasons.

Connah's Quay is one of the best places on the estuary to see a variety of birds of prey attracted by the great numbers of small waders and landbirds. Outside the breeding season, one or two Peregrines and several Merlins may also be seen. In addition, an occasional Rough-legged Buzzard and Marsh Harrier hunt during migration, and Sparrowhawks, Barn Owls and Little Owls are present throughout the year. There are also good numbers of Short-eared Owls, Kestrels and Herons and an occasional migrant Hen Harrier; their main prey is the abundant Short-tailed Field Vole. Common, Arctic and Little Terns roost on the reserve and feed on small fish offshore at high-tide.

The reserve can be reached from the A548. Non-members of the Deeside Naturalists' Society may visit at weekends by prior arrangement with the Station Manager, Connah's Quay Power Station, Connah's Quay, Deeside.

CHAPTER NINE

Leighton Moss and
Morecambe Bay Reserves
RSPB

These two important reserves although almost adjoining are in total contrast. Taken together, they comprise one of the most rewarding birdwatching areas in Britain; and they are right next door to the popular resort of Morecambe with its 42,000 inhabitants. The huge bay and inlet are bounded by the coastlines of south Cumbria and north Lancashire and five rivers (Wyre, Lune, Keer, Kent and Leven) join the sea here. Morecambe lies on the southeast shore of the bay looking across to the distant Cumbrian mountains, which form the backdrop to the Lake District. There is all the fun-of-the-fair to be found in the holiday town, yet, just a short walk away, at the northern end of the promenade, it is possible to feast the eyes on one of the finest bird spectaculars in Europe. At low-tide, the 120 square miles of mud and sand provide the perfect feeding ground for tens of thousands of waders, wildfowl, gulls and terns. The reserves are administered as one from the Reception Centre at Leighton Moss.

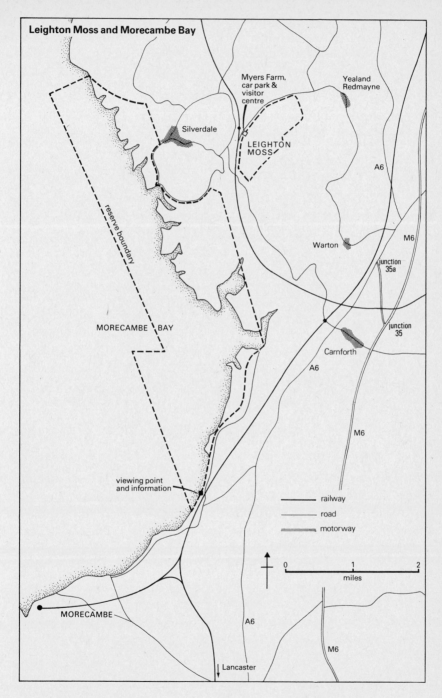

Leighton Moss and Morecambe Bay

Myers Farm,
car park &
visitor
centre

Yealand
Redmayne

Silverdale

LEIGHTON
MOSS

A6

reserve boundary

Warton

M6

junction
35a

MORECAMBE BAY

junction
35

Carnforth

A6

M6

viewing point
and information

railway
road
motorway

0   1   2
miles

MORECAMBE

A6

M6

Lancaster

Leighton Moss

The reserve lies just back from the sea, near the northeast tip of the bay between the villages of Silverdale and Yealand Redmayne. The word Moss derives from the Old English 'Mos' meaning a swamp. It first became an RSPB reserve in 1964, when it was leased from the owners of Leighton Hall. The final purchase was made in 1974. Whereas Morecambe Bay's 6000 acres make it the largest reserve in RSPB ownership, Leighton Moss with 400 is one of the smallest. It lies in a pleasant wooded valley and several small springs and streams drain into it from the surrounding limestone hills.

At one time the Moss was reclaimed for agriculture by a system of dykes and a steam-pump, but this was discontinued during the First World War and soon several small meres formed. The valley floor consists of a layer of peat on maritime clay, so ideal conditions existed for the growth of reeds and willow scrub, and in a short time the largest reed-bed in northern England had developed. It is especially important because this type of habitat has now become one of Britain's scarcest.

The main management problem is to control the spread of the reeds, otherwise, in a few decades, helped by willows and alders, they would dry out the land. Before long the result would be an oak forest. The reeds are controlled by spraying and cutting; local plants have been introduced, new meres formed and many artificial islands built for nesting birds. As a result, about 50 species breed here each year from a check-list of nearly 200 which have been recorded. The reeds now cover half the reserve and in some places grow 10 feet high. Large stands of brilliant yellow flags and reedmace, the common bulrush or cat's tail, break the sea of green.

Thanks to these 200 acres of reeds, Leighton Moss has become the only place left in northern Britain where that strange bird, the Bittern, can still breed. There is now a stable population of from ten to twelve pairs here. The best time to see them is in early summer, when there are young about, and the parent birds are forced to forage for food. These tawny and gold relations of the Heron hunt in the thick cover of the reeds. With luck, you might suddenly see one emerge stealthily from cover in pursuit of a small mammal or frog or some other choice item of prey. If alarmed, it will freeze with its dagger-like bill pointed to the sky and at once become almost invisible against the background of reeds. In hard winters when the marshes are iced over or covered in snow they suffer greatly. Fortunately, in this sheltered valley near the northwest coast warmed by the Gulf Stream, they enjoy exceptionally mild conditions. For this reason they are heard booming from the middle of January until mid-summer – a week or two earlier than at their East Anglian stronghold.

The other star bird on the reserve, also dependent on the cover of reeds, is the Bearded Tit or Bearded Reedling. A small colony established itself here in 1973. This elegant little bird, mainly tawny-orange in colour with a long rounded tail, black moustachial stripes and lavender-grey head, does not in fact belong to the titmouse family, but is a unique species in Europe and is related to the parrotbills of southern China. Like Bitterns, they suffer in hard winters but are able to recover numbers rapidly as they are prolific breeders and in long, warm summers may have as many as four broods. They are now numerous in the East Anglian marshes and are spreading out to other areas of reed-bed in England, but the most northerly point they have reached is here at Leighton Moss.

There are several wooden hides which give good opportunities for seeing many of the breeding birds. Reed Warblers, Sedge Warblers and Reed Buntings are common. Another summer resident is the Grasshopper Warbler, but he tries to stay out of sight and can often only be detected by the sound of his strange song, which sounds like an angler casting his line or perhaps a bicycle freewheeling. There are Black-headed Gulls in large numbers, but only the very sharp-eyed will see that marvellously camouflaged game-bird the Woodcock. The elusive Water Rails do well here, but are more often heard than seen. Their calls vary through a range of grunts and clicks to a blood-curdling squeal, like a stuck pig: a puzzling sound from the reeds in spring.

Wildfowl breed in good numbers with Mallard, Teal, Shoveler and Tufted Duck the most common. Kestrels, Sparrowhawks and Barn Owls nest close by and frequently hunt over the reserve. The best time to see them is in late summer and autumn, when tens of thousands of Starlings roost in the reeds. And at the autumn migration there are great spectacles and good hunting for the birds of prey; at this time Swallows and Sand Martins gather in their thousands with smaller flocks of Pied and Yellow Wagtails.

The reed-beds should be able to provide the right breeding conditions for Marsh Harriers, but usually only a rare visitor is seen in late spring. This may be because the Bitterns have made the reeds their stronghold. Single Ospreys, usually young birds, probably from Scotland, appear most years and often remain for weeks.

Autumn sees the passage of waders, though not in great numbers. A wide variety, including Spotted Redshank, Greenshank and Ruff, stay to feed in the shallow water right in front of the hides. Winter brings the visiting wildfowl: mainly thousands of Teal and Mallard, but also small numbers of Widgeon, Pintail, Shoveler, Pochard, Tufted Duck and Goldeneye.

In addition to the birds, Leighton Moss is one of the best reserves to see that attractive creature, now sadly declining in numbers in many parts of the country, the Otter. Here the water is free from pollution and Otters are given full protection. They usually move through the water with an undulating movement of head, body and tail, which sometimes make it difficult to be certain just how many are present. On occasions five adults have been seen together. When the water is rough, their undulations might appear to be those of some curious monster, which might possibly explain some of those annual sightings on certain lochs in Scotland. Rather surprisingly the cubs do not swim instinctively, but have to be taught by their parents.

Of the larger mammals, Red and Roe Deer often seek sanctuary in the reed-beds; Fallow Deer are also seen occasionally. It is also good to know that Red Squirrels continue to survive in neighbouring woods.

Leighton Moss is also an excellent place for insects and over 300 species of moth have been recorded, including the Large and Small Elephant Hawk Moth. Among the many butterflies, the most common are Peacocks seen on willow catkins in spring and among the red and purple of hemp agrimony and knapweed in autumn. Brimstones are attracted by alder buckthorn, and among many typical species are the Orange Tip and Meadow Brown, which are to be found on the drier parts of the fen. Among the limestone outcrops at the north end of the reserve, Pearl-bordered and High Brown Fritillaries may be seen.

Before leaving the reserve, it is advisable to enquire at the Reception Centre – in an old stone barn – about the times of the tides for Morecambe Bay.

Access Off the A6, 8 miles north of Lancaster, thence via Yealand Redmayne. There is a car park for visitors. The reserve is also easily accessible by rail; it is only a short walk from Silverdale station.
Opening times From 10 a.m. to 4 p.m. on the following days: April to September: Saturday, Sunday, Wednesday, Thursday; October to January: Wednesday, Sunday; February to March: Wednesday, Saturday, Sunday.
Permit Obtainable on the reserve.
Facilities Large reception/interpretive centre and shop. There are five hides, including one permanently available free on public right of way across the centre of the reserve. Warm clothing is advisable.
Warden Leighton Moss, Silverdale, Lancashire.

Morecambe Bay

We now come to the wide open spaces of the bay itself, where at low-tide the mud and sand stretch away to the distant Cumbrian Hills. (No wonder that a person born in Morecambe is known locally as a 'sangronun' – meaning someone who has been born in the sand.) The first thing is to check the time and height of the tide; then the best plan is to walk northward along the shore from the end of the town promenade to Hest Bank at the southern tip of the reserve. A good time is $1\frac{1}{2}$ hours before high tide. Here, close to a public car park, can be seen one of the biggest wader roosts in Europe. The birds feed on the tiny creatures in the 120 square miles of sandflats which provide a vast, natural store of food. This is all the more vital now when throughout Europe, industrial development and reclamation for agriculture are increasingly taking place over flat coasts and estuaries. At least here, the RSPB has been able to secure a roosting and feeding place for tens of thousands of birds on their great journeyings across the world.

At Hest Bank there are splendid viewing sites, where one causes no disturbance to the huge flocks, and, as high-tide approaches, the birds become even more closely packed. In winter there may be up to 60,000 waders – Knot, Dunlin, Curlew, Redshank and Oystercatcher, with smaller flocks of Bar-tailed Godwit and other species.

As the tide recedes, it is possible to walk through the shore-side saltings of sea meadow-grass and fescue, but it is not advisable to go too far towards the sea as there is a network of pools and creeks, known locally as gutters, stretching across the sands.

At the peak times of spring and autumn migration, the roosts become even larger. The most spectacular time of all is in early May, when the locally-feeding birds are joined by Ringed Plovers, Sanderlings, Whimbrels and others, which have wintered further south, swelling the total of waders to upward of 100,000. Peregrines find the roosts rewarding hunting-grounds and, as soon as one of these raptors appears, there is panic, especially among the smaller birds. Flocks of Knot and Dunlin swirl like great clouds of smoke and produce changing patterns in the sky as they wheel and twist to avoid the deadly menace of the Peregrine's stoops. Merlins also winter here and the little falcons can often be seen in characteristic dashing flight.

Wildfowl use the reserve as a daytime roost, flying in from Leighton Moss and other inland areas. At peak winter periods there may be 2000 Mallard and Widgeon, and several hundred Teal, Pintail and Shoveler. Shelduck are numerous and build up to 2000 in mid-winter. In June and July, the estuary of the River Keer, in the centre of the reserve area, is a gathering place for large flocks of adult Shelducks before they head away inland, bound eventually for the Heligoland Bight area of Germany, where they carry out their annual moult. Flocks of Greylag and Pink-footed Geese occasionally fly over or land on the saltings, when they have been disturbed from their grazing fields. Scaup, Red-breasted Mergansers and Goldeneyes, sometimes even a Long-tailed Duck, may be identified among rafts of wildfowl lying offshore at high-tide.

Access To Hest Bank viewing sites via A5105, 4 miles north of Morecambe. Walk across the railway line and follow the track northward along the saltings' edge. Cars may be parked near the level crossing, where there are excellent views. (For other details see Leighton Moss.)

Other sites:

Bardsea Cumbria County Council

This pleasant country park on the opposite shore of the bay from the RSPB reserves is 2 miles south of Ulverston on the A5087. It has a well-sited car park and offers woodland and seaside bird habitats as well as good views of waders roosting at high-tide.

South Walney Island, Cumbria Cumbria Naturalists' Trust

The southern half of this narrow, 9-mile-long island at the western entrance to Morecambe Bay holds Europe's largest colony of gulls. In this sanctuary, close to a residential area and much-used beaches, and near the busy industrial port of Barrow-in-Furness, some 50,000 pairs of Herring and Lesser Black-backed Gulls nest on the dunes. There are also small numbers of Great Black-backed Gulls, which are even more predatory than their smaller relatives. Most important of all, a breeding colony of Eiders, now some 400 pairs, has developed here since 1949 and flourishes in spite of being surrounded by gulls. This is the only nesting colony of the northern sea-duck on England's west coast. Outside the breeding season, the tip of Walney Island and its neighbouring Piel Island, which is tiny and adorned with a castle, provide roosting grounds for spectacular numbers of waders. There are also excellent points for viewing birds feeding in Morecambe Bay or moving up and down this eastern section of the Irish Sea.

For a permit to visit the sanctuary write to: South Walney Nature Reserve, Barrow, Cumbria. Cross the bridge to the island from Barrow-in-Furness reached on the A590 from Ulverston by the side of which, *en route*, can be seen the splendid remains of the Red Sandstone 12th-century Furness Abbey. Alternatively, along the scenic A5867 coastal road from Ulverston via Bardsea where, 1 mile west, are a ruined temple and prehistoric stone circles.

In addition to the delights of birdwatching, this area of northwest England has much to offer. Lancaster is only 4 miles away and well repays a visit. The Romans gave Lancashire's county town its name, when they first set up a camp here by the River Lune. There is a magnificent castle dating back to the Normans, a 14th-century parish church; and in the Market Square, Charles II was proclaimed king in 1651.

Above all, Morecambe is within easy reach of the incomparably beautiful Lake District. Windermere is just 30 miles away and beyond lie Ambleside and the famous Langdale Pikes, Grasmere and Keswick with their memories of Wordsworth, Shelley and Ruskin. Few areas of Britain can offer such a wealth of scenic beauty combined with historic and wildlife interest.

CHAPTER TEN

St Bees Head, Cumbria
RSPB

The red cliffs jut into the Irish Sea opposite the northern tip of the Isle of Man; just 4 miles up the Cumbrian coast is the industrial port of Whitehaven. The harbour here saw a strange happening during the American War of Independence. In 1778 the dashing sea captain Paul Jones, who had served his apprenticeship as a seaman at Whitehaven, sailed into the harbour in command of an American brig and shot up three boats. Today, 360 feet up on the cliff top nothing disturbs the calm, save the wild cries of thousands of breeding seabirds; a short distance inland, there stretches all the scenic beauty of England's matchless Lake District.

The structure of the great outcrop of sandstone is ideal for providing ledges on the cliff-face to accommodate the nesting birds. St Bees has the largest seabird colony on the west coast, numbering well over 5000 pairs, and much of it can be seen in the course of a gentle walk along the flower-strewn cliff path.

It is also distinguished for being the only mainland breeding place in England of the Black Guillemot. The Tystie, as it is known in the north, unlike the other members of the auk family – the Guillemot, Razorbill and Puffin – nests low down in crevices among the boulders or in caves. At St Bees there are usually five or six pairs. They are easy to spot from the cliff top thanks to their distinctive white wing patches and bright scarlet legs and feet. These show up clearly as the rest of their plumage is blackish-brown. Tysties also differ from the other auks in normally laying two eggs, as opposed to the single egg of its relatives. The total breeding population of Black Guillemots for Britain and Ireland is somewhere between 8000 and 9000 pairs, the majority of which are in Orkney and Shetland.

The most numerous breeding bird here is the Common Guillemot of which there are usually at least 2500 pairs. It is their strange growling notes and the cries of the Kittiwakes that make up most of the wild chorus of sound. There are also excellent views of Fulmars, which often breed on ledges near the top of the cliff. They will even allow a close approach to be made to the nest as they fix the intruder with their dark, deep-set eyes. Undue liberties are highly inadvisable as, if provoked, the bird can eject an oily spew which jets out for several feet with a singularly noisome stench. This highly effective defence mechanism gave the bird its name, which means 'foul gull'. The cliffs also hold a several-thousand-strong colony of Herring Gulls.

Apart from seabirds, there are a few Kestrels and Ravens. There is also a good chance of seeing Stonechats perched on the tops of bushes flirting their tails as they utter a squeaky little song. Approach close to them and they give a sharp alarm call, which sounds just like two pebbles being knocked together – hence the name. The male is certainly eye-catching with his glossy black head, white collar and rich chestnut-coloured breast.

The RSPB now owns several miles of the cliff top on the North and South Heads and there is a public footpath with signposted observation points. No cliff climbing is allowed during the summer. It is important not to damage or clamber over fences as they are there to stop farm animals straying and falling over the cliffs. The terrain is suitable for family visits.

To reach the Head, turn off the A595 for St Bees village. The cliff-top path can be reached from the beach at St Bees or from Sandwith Village. Cars must not be driven up the private road to the cliffs from Sandwith. There is a warden from April to August based at the Leighton Moss Reserve. (See page 71.)

CHAPTER ELEVEN

Handa Reserve, Sutherland
RSPB

The island of Handa is only just offshore, one of a myriad little pieces of the shattered Atlantic edge of Scotland's northwestern mountains. It is remote nevertheless, and not the least of its attractions is getting there, even to the boat-quay at Tarbet where the island is less than a mile away across bird-filled waters. The road to Scourie, the nearest village, comes up through Wester Ross into Sutherland, winding around the finger-tips of sea lochs that have found their way into high purple hills. There are little islets, deserted castles and empty bays of shining white sand. It is all very quiet, peaceful and unexploited, for the Gulf Stream, this far north, has cooled a bit and is only for the hardiest swimmers.

Although it can be reached by a short journey in a little boat – and the birdwatcher could wish it were longer with so many sea ducks, auks, gulls and terns to be seen – Handa is full of the atmosphere of isolation. More or less round in shape, and with a surface of 766 acres, the island is a tilted chunk of Torridonian Sandstone. The boat lands at a low sandy bay which faces the mainland and slopes upwards across boggy heaths and grassland to

400-foot cliffs that drop sheer into the Atlantic. Due west across the ocean, past the northern tip of the Outer Hebrides, is Labrador.

An RSPB warden and usually one or two voluntary helpers are resident for the summer and spend their days out in the field guarding and recording the separate numbers and behaviour of the 100,000 birds, of some 30 species, that nest on the island. The visitor-centre, an old stone building up on the slope above the landing point, provides full details of Handa's wildlife and the self-guided trail. Boardwalks cover the wettest sections of the path, which leads upwards across the centre of the island to the very edge of the cliffs then back via a bay on the south coast.

The visitor should not stray, if only to avoid being attacked by skuas. About twenty-five pairs of Bonxies (Great Skuas) and about half that number of Arctic Skuas nest in the heather and grass of the central slopes and are seen extremely well on either side of the trail. Handa is probably the most accessible of the British nesting sites of these two species, and with complete protection on this island each has been steadily increasing its numbers since they returned to breed here in the 1960s. The larger Bonxie is a predator, killing smaller sea birds and also preying on their eggs and chicks, while the more lightly-built Arctic Skua is piratical, patrolling opportunistically offshore and forcing gulls, terns and Puffins to disgorge or drop fish they are taking back to their nests.

Skuas look like dark brown immature gulls but they are markedly different in silhouette, having narrower wings, bent back at the wrist, and wedge-shaped tails with long central feathers. Handa's Arctic Skua is easily differentiated from the heavy, all-brown Bonxie by its black cap, pale collar, longer tail projections and white underparts showing up well, though a few Arctics may have dark bodies. Its present increase, though slow, is one of conservation's success stories. Once common and more widespread, its numbers were greatly reduced by persecution until protection of the species and, especially, its habitat, began to be enforced. The population throughout its breeding range in the north, however, has only just exceeded 1000 pairs and it is still the rarest seabird nesting in the British Isles.

Handa's present inhabitants, the wardens, no longer eat seabirds and their eggs as, no doubt, did members of the seven families who eked out an existence on the island until 1848. Some of these hardy people lie buried in a little graveyard which can still be seen near the visitors' hut.

The steadily rising walk up to the cliff edge is rewarded at the end with resting places of soft turf among clumps of pink thrift and white campion. Suddenly, here, one is in another world. From these lofty perches, with the white-frothed, blue-green sea far below, there are dramatic views of thousands of seabirds nesting on narrow ledges of the cliffs and the Stack or wheeling in masses in the up-currents. On this short stretch of Handa's high coast are crammed some 25,000 pairs of Guillemots, 9000 pairs of Razorbills, 13,000 pairs of Kittiwakes, 3500 pairs of Fulmars and 400 pairs of Shags. Dispersed in holes near the cliff tops, or standing around in silent little groups, are up to 500 pairs of Puffins. A few hundred pairs of Herring Gulls and fifty pairs of Great Black-backed Gulls are much in evidence as, predatory like the skuas, they look for unguarded eggs and chicks or injured birds. In this wild environment, it seems incongruous to see real, wild Rock Doves, the species from which the world's town pigeons were developed.

Continuing the trail and leaving the noisy cliffs is like closing the door on a city in the rush hour. The gently-falling slopes of heather and grass, where spotted heath orchids add extra colour, are given over only to Rabbits, silent, staring Sheep and to little birds with little voices. Here and there, a Skylark sings its way into the heavens, a Meadow Pipit rises and falls on a trilling song-flight and a cock Wheatear chacks harshly, flirting its black and white tail. Occasionally a Snipe drums and, more rarely, a Golden Plover, spangled and almost invisible against the heather, calls plaintively, asking to be left alone. The little, dark-headed, Robin-shaped bird watching from the top of a gorse bush is a Stonechat.

Down at the shore, soon reached, the birdwatcher can sit again to look and listen at leisure. Among the boulders and on the short turf up from the high-water line, Oystercatchers, Ringed Plovers and Lapwings nest. A few Common Terns and Common Gulls fly ashore. They also nest here, as do the Eiders and Shelducks which can easily be identified as they float placidly on the waters of the bay.

Around the coast and more certainly in the quieter narrows between the island and the mainland, Black Guillemots are to be seen. They do not nest on Handa but are a regular and interesting addition to the birdwatcher's list. Here, too, Red-throated Divers may be seen on the water or flying in, hunch-backed and stiff-winged, from further out at sea where they more usually prefer to fish. A very few pairs nest on the banks of some of the reserve's half-dozen lochans, but they are 'Schedule 1' species, specially protected by law, and their nesting areas are out of bounds. Breeding only in northwest Scotland, with a few pairs also in northwest Ireland, this diver is steadily spreading back into its once much-wider range now that it is less persecuted: many fishermen could not tolerate competition from this bird. The most recent survey by the British Trust for Ornithology shows, however, that the number of Red-throated Divers breeding in Britain is still fewer than 800 pairs.

The Red-throat is the smallest of four species of divers, large water birds that catch fish in the sea or large lakes by submerging from the surface. To be able to do this and to swim most efficiently under the water, they have big webbed feet, set far back on the body. This special adaptation is achieved at the expense of agility on land. Because it walks with difficulty and often resorts to shuffling along on its breast, the Red-throat sites its nest on the very edge of a lochan which is often just large enough to act as a landing-strip. The bird does not need a long length of water since it lands on its well-padded underparts and stops quickly, unlike swans and ducks which skid along on their feet.

The red patch on the throat of this diver is small, really only visible at close range, and is moulted after the breeding season. At a distance, the species can be distinguished from the slightly larger Black-throated Diver, which can also be seen in the north, and from the rare, still larger Great Northern, by its uptilted bill. At closer range, the absence of noticeable white spots on its back is also a helpful feature.

Handa boasts one little copse, a plantation of lodgepole pines and alders which struggle for existence against the salty wind near the warden's bothy. Small night migrants like warblers and thrushes, grounded by bad weather, soon make for this cover, and many a rarity has been seen here. Larger, more obvious and quite frequent visitors to the island are Buzzards, Peregrines and Sparrowhawks. A Golden Eagle may also wander across from the mainland, but only rarely. At sea, the passage past the island can be spectacular, with large numbers and a wide variety of birds, especially Greylag and Pink-footed Geese, heading north in spring for their breeding grounds.

There is a lot to see on Handa. If a part-day visit does not satisfy the get-away-from-it-all type of birdwatcher, he or she could try a week or more of residence in the bothy as a volunteer assistant. The warden is glad of help with his duties and does not like being lonely.

Access By boat from Tarbet. Take the minor road down to the water's edge at Tarbet, eastwards off the A894, half-way between Laxford Bridge and Scourie. Warm clothing is recommended.

Opening times Local fishermen operate small boats, at no fixed times, from April to the end of September. No permit required.

Accommodation There are two hotels and two B & B guest-houses in Scourie. Full details of accommodation throughout the area (send 25p postage) from: Wester Ross Tourist Organization, Tourist Office, Gairloch, Ross-shire IV21 2DN; telephone Gairloch (0445) 75605. Or from Sutherland Tourist Organization, Area Tourist Office, The Square, Dornoch, Sutherland IV25 3SD; telephone Dornoch (086 281) 400.

Information leaflet about Handa and enquiries about staying on the island as a voluntary warden from: RSPB Scottish Office, 17 Regent Terrace, Edinburgh EH7 5BN; Tel: (031) 556 5624.

CHAPTER TWELVE

Orkney, the RSPB Reserves

There is a distinct sense of exhilaration on setting out for the northern isles. Perhaps, because they are shown boxed-off in a corner of the map, we think of them as being apart and different. And so they are – in many ways. For 500 years the islands came under Scandinavian rule and it was not until the 15th century that they were ceded to Scotland. The Norse imprint is therefore strong; and scenically, too, there is a total contrast with the Highlands.

Orkney is a gentle landscape of low hills 'like sleeping whales' and, not surprisingly in this fertile land, cattle farming is the main industry. There are few trees: the Orcadians say 'usually trees shelter houses, here houses shelter trees'. Above all, there is a marvellous light: the clean, clear air is a pleasure to breathe; and on summer nights it is never really dark.

In all, there are about sixty islands, bunched in three groups from northwest to southeast over a distance of 50 miles. Only twenty-two are inhabited and the total population is no more than 18,000.

The two great attractions of Orkney are the mysterious, archaeological sites and, of course, the birds. For birdwatchers the ideal time for a visit is between mid-May and early July, when there is one of the greatest seabird spectacles to be seen anywhere in Europe: a million seabirds in their breeding colonies, that is, one-sixth of the British total, and, including landbirds, some ninety species will be present.

To get to Orkney there is the choice of flying to Kirkwall and hiring a car at the airport or taking one's own across on the P. and O. Ferry MV *St Ola* from Scrabster. This covers the 27 miles to Stromness in the southwest corner, in two hours, first sailing across the narrow and sometimes turbulent waters of the Pentland Firth. Before long, the Isle of Hoy is seen on the starboard bow, together with the unmistakable gaunt silhouette of the Old Man of Hoy – that freakish, splintered tower of rock rising to 450 feet and presenting a supreme test to rock climbers.

The name Hoy means 'high island' and indeed the cliffs at St John's Head on the northwest coast rise to an awesome 1100 feet. At the extreme northern end, the summit of Ward Hill towers to more than 1500 feet and is by far the highest point in the whole of Orkney. Seabirds flicker white against the sombre cliffs and there might even be a glimpse of a soaring Golden Eagle or a Peregrine.

All around are birds seldom seen in the south – the piratical Great and Arctic Skuas, Black Guillemots with white wing patches flashing in low, whirring flight, Puffins splashing the waves with their wings, bright orange feet twinkling, placid-looking Eiders and the graceful Arctic Terns. Among them, there might even be a rare Glaucous or Iceland Gull.

This host of birds provides a fitting escort as the *St Ola* leaves Hoy behind and approaches Mainland and the compact little port of Stromness. First impressions are of a jumble of bright-painted fishing boats, orange sandstone houses and grey jetties set against a backcloth of gardens on a granite hillside.

The Vikings called this largest of the islands Hrossey, or Horse Island; now, we know it more prosaically as Mainland. It stretches 23 miles across and the two ends are joined by the narrow waist of the Scapa isthmus. This is where the capital Kirkwall is situated; the great deep-water anchorage of Scapa Flow, famous in two world wars, lies across the isthmus to the south.

One of the RSPB's most important Orkney reserves is at

Marwick Head on the northwestern coast. From Kirkwall it is about 15 miles over a good, though narrow, road to reach the rock-strewn bay of Mar Wick. There is no reserve warden, but the path up to the cliff-edge over the peaty turf is clearly shown and is bright with clumps of campion and thrift. The cliffs are dangerous in places and great care must be taken not to stray from the path. Down the cliff-face, Arctic Skuas from nearby breeding colonies can be seen raiding seabird nests in attempts to snatch the defenceless young. The sound is stupendous as a screeching cloud of birds tries to ward off the marauders. Sometimes, down on the surface of the sea, a Great Skua can be seen tearing at the corpse of a Guillemot; other members of the auk family float around in an impotent circle, unable to prevent the grisly feast.

Half-way along the path to the cliff top, look out for the number '129' painted on a rock face. This indicates a good vantage point from which to get a close view of the breeding colonies. Kittiwakes are the noisiest – forever crying their names – kittee-wayke. Thanks to present-day protection, these gentle-looking gulls have greatly increased their numbers and 500,000 pairs now breed around our coasts. The thin layers of hard and soft rock can be clearly seen in the Old Red Sandstone of Marwick Head. The soft sandstone, paler in colour, has eroded to provide ledges on which seabirds can select their favoured nesting sites.

Kittiwakes choose precarious ledges, as narrow as 6 inches, for their clutch of two or three eggs; yet the nests are large and straggly. The Guillemots use long, narrow, flat ledges, and lay the single egg direct on the rock. The egg is considerably more pointed at one end than the other, so that if given an accidental nudge, it simply rolls round in a half-circle instead of toppling into the sea. The Razorbills are less numerous and lay their rounder egg in deep crevices. Fulmars and a very few Ravens nest on the wider ledges; Jackdaws and Puffins use holes.

On the uplands, streaky-brown Twites breed in the heather. They look very like Linnets, but the males have no red on breast or forehead. Here too nest the dapper Wheatears, white rumps flashing as they fly. Up on the cliff summit, towering overall, is a monument to Lord Kitchener of Khartoum, the British Commander-in-Chief in the First World War. While carrying him on a mission to Russia in 1916, the cruiser HMS *Hampshire* struck a mine off the nearby Brough of Birsay and sank with only a handful of survivors. A pinnacle of rock nearby is a lonely vantage point for a Peregrine.

For moorland birds, the principal RSPB reserve is at Hobbister, 5 miles southwest of Kirkwall and overlooking Scapa Flow. Early in the last war, a German U-boat slipped through the defences and sank HMS *Royal Oak*. It was then decided to erect barriers across the eastern entrance, and five small islands to the south were joined together by a road on a massive concrete embankment. Another Scapa Flow island – Flotta – is now a terminal for North Sea Oil. Fortunately, in Orkney there is not very much evidence of the vast new industry, although here the gas flare throws a baleful light across the winter skies. Inevitably, the thousands of seabirds feeding offshore are now under serious threat. With the many oil tankers and other vessels crowding these waters oil slicks are bound to occur from time to time.

This reserve above Scapa was established to protect a rare landbird – the Hen Harrier. Orkney is its most important breeding area in Britain and usually about five females have nests at Hobbister. The males are polygamous and sometimes cope with three, or even as many as five mates. The reasons for its stronghold here are complex but may be linked with an abundance of food: that unique little mammal the Orkney Vole no doubt figures on the menu.

The 1800-acre reserve is leased from the Highland Park Distillery, which has been established at Kirkwall since 1798 and cuts its peat here. It is best approached from Waulkmill Bay where cars may be parked. As Hen Harriers are by law a specially protected species, their nests must not be disturbed and access is restricted to the public paths, which meander over the boggy heath between the bay and the A964 main road.

Until the 18th century, the 'ash-coloured hawks' were widespread in the British Isles, but relentless persecution by gamekeepers and the reclamation of moorland eventually restricted them to Orkney and the Outer Hebrides. For some time now they have been recolonizing the Scottish mainland and even moving back, sparingly, to northern and midland England and the uplands of Wales.

It is an unforgettable experience to watch the Hen Harriers in their rugged, moorland setting. The males are strikingly handsome, especially when seen with their broad wings gleaming silvery-grey in pale sun. The wingbeats are slow and heavy; with each downstroke the jet black wing tips are clearly seen. Females are bigger and have a different plumage – a mixture of browns and greys with a white rump. The males are most often seen gliding a few feet above the peat bogs as they patiently quarter the heather. Seen at close quarters, the hawk's head is surprisingly owl-like with staring, yellow-rimmed eyes.

During the breeding season, there is a chance of seeing the food-pass aerobatics. Incubation of the four to six eggs lasts about thirty days and is carried out by the female. The male does most of the hunting and, on his return over the nest site, the female often flies up steeply towards him, flips over momentarily on her back, and the prey is then passed unerringly from talon to talon. There are variations of the pass: the male may drop the prey from his claws and the female, flying below and behind him, will then seize it as it falls. The recovery in numbers of the Hen Harrier has been a considerable conservation success story.

Hobbister has a few pairs of Merlins – those dashing little falcons with long, narrow wings and tails – also Kestrels and Short-eared Owls, which hunt the Orkney Voles by day. Red Grouse, Curlews, Snipe, Redshanks and Common Gulls nest in the peatbog and heather. Among the smaller birds, often perched on a clump of creeping willow or a sprig of crowberry, are the orange-breasted Stonechats, forever flicking their tails. Down at Waulkmill Bay and out on the loch there are numbers of Tufted Duck, Eider and Shelduck.

This is also a likely place to see a Red-breasted Merganser, one of the saw-billed diving ducks. The serrations along the edges of the bill mean that a slippery fish can be gripped with ease. The drake has a distinctive untidy crest on its bottle-green head, a chestnut-coloured breast and grey and white back. Red-throated Divers may well be gracing the waters of Loch Kirbister. The red throat-patch is present in summer only, but there is no mistaking that weird reptilian appearance of a diver and, unlike the Black-throats, the bill is rather thin and uptilted.

There is botanical interest here too: on the wet heath the yellow stars of bog asphodel are found and the insect-catching sundew. Many kinds of orchid also flourish on this excellent moorland reserve.

Another RSPB reserve on Mainland with Hen Harriers and heathland birds is the Dale of Cottasgarth in Rendall. This was Orkney's first reserve and forms part of a large area of moors classified as Grade I by the Nature Conservancy Council. Here, by the kind permission of the farmer, cars may be parked at Lower Cottasgarth. It is important to keep to the path leading to the Dale. Care should also be taken to close gates and no dogs are allowed. There is a good viewpoint from the ruined farm buildings at Dale.

Although most of Orkney's birds can be seen on Mainland, it is well worth visiting the other islands too, and for seabirds the Noup Cliffs on the northwest coast of Westray are particularly rewarding. From Kirkwall airport, situated serenely by the side of a calm bay facing north, the eight-seater Islanders of Loganair provide an excellent service. To reach Westray means flying over the vivid-green island of Shapinsay, past Rousay, and out across the Firth. The Noup Cliffs are a short drive from the airfield by hired car arranged in advance or, if preferred, it is a pleasant walk.

The RSPB owns $1\frac{1}{2}$ miles of the cliff top and a strip of land between Noup Head and Monivey. This is a remote, wild corner of northern Britain and there are unforgettable breath-taking sights of the awesome, creviced cliff-face with its vast population of seabirds. Guillemots stand shoulder to shoulder – a recent count estimated their numbers at 40,000 – and their strange growling sounds fill the air. The next most numerous are the Kittiwakes with about 25,000 pairs. Razorbills, Puffins, Fulmars and Shags are present in smaller numbers. One of the most dramatic viewpoints is at Kelda Ber.

Back to the airfield for a last hop north. This time, to the tiny island of Papa Westray, which can be clearly seen across a narrow strip of sea. That is as far north as Orkney goes. The crossing is by boat or by the shortest scheduled air flight in the world – as listed in *The Guinness Book of Records*. It takes exactly two minutes to flip across, before landing on an airfield, which is little more than a strip of thickish grass: there is only a huddle of huts and a windsock;

Corncrakes rasp unseen. The island is only $4\frac{1}{2}$ miles long by 1 mile wide and the 100 inhabitants live by stock farming and fishing. The name is pronounced 'pappy' and it derives from 'Pappae', the priests of the early Celtic Church who settled here. The RSPB reserve is at North Hill overlooking the sea. It is managed by agreement with the islanders, who graze their cattle on the close-cropped grass and heather, interspersed with creeping willow and crowberry. Alpine flowers can be found at about 500 feet, and there are large groups of one of the north's special flowers, the tiny, red Scots primrose.

Conditions on Papa Westray are ideal for Arctic Terns and, most years, there is a huge colony of 5000 to 6000 pairs, who find an abundant supply of small fish around the island. They are fierce in defence of their eggs and chicks and will not hesitate to dive-bomb and scare away cattle or sheep if they stray too close to their breeding ground. Two-legged intruders will also be attacked and bare heads may soon be bleeding. It is a forcible reminder not to stray from the path and, no wonder, the local name for Arctic Terns is 'Pickies'.

Close by in the heather is a colony of some 100 pairs of the larger and even more aggressive Arctic Skuas. These brown and white pirates with hooked bills prey on the terns, forcing them to drop food in mid-flight, or often raid a nest to snatch an unguarded chick. Down on the rocky shore, Black Guillemots nest under boulders.

At the southeast corner of the reserve, there is a higher stretch of cliffs known as Fowl Craig. Mist swirls up a cleft here like steam from a cauldron and, in winter, storm-lashed seas even explode over the cliff top, 50 feet above. Nearby is a small cave where what might well have been the very last of the Great Auks was shot in 1813. This flightless bird, $2\frac{1}{2}$ feet tall, which used its tiny wings only for swimming, now rests as a stuffed skin in the British Natural History Museum. It is a prized item in the collection and a tragic warning of what might have happened to other species had protection not been forthcoming in the nick of time.

There is a small loch on the island and a rarity for several years was a Steller's Eider drake, a straggler from Arctic Siberia or perhaps Alaska. He was in the company of a small flock of Eider; distinctive, his pale upperparts contrasting with black on back and neck. The breast was reddish-brown and he showed it proudly in display, although the other Eiders seemed not at all impressed. There was sadly little chance of his ever finding a mate.

At one time, that skulking migrant, the Corncrake, nested in most of Britain, especially where there was long grass grown for hay. But it sits close and with today's earlier harvesting by fast machines instead of by hand-scythe in July which saved the habitat and allowed a sympathetic farm-worker to spare a nest or brood of chicks, most of its safe breeding areas in England and Wales have been lost. The once familiar rasping call, which inspired Linnaeus to give it the scientific name of *Crex crex*, is now confined to the north-west of Britain and much of Ireland, especially on islands, and you will not fail to hear it here on Papa Westray in late spring or summer.

It would be unthinkable to leave Orkney without taking a look at some of the numerous archaeological sites. Here, on the lonely western shore of Papa Westray, is the Knap of Howar, consisting of two roofless houses of stone. They stand in a hollow dug into a grassy slope running down to the sea and are probably Europe's oldest standing dwellings. Alongside, there is a midden of bones and oystershells left by the mysterious Stone Age inhabitants some 5000 years ago. They no doubt also lived on the Common and Grey Seals which abound round the island.

Back on Mainland off the B9056, 6 miles north of Stromness, on the shore of Skaill Bay, is an entire Stone Age village: the famous Skara Brae. Like Pompeii, it was hit by a natural calamity; only in this case it was storm-driven sand. It remained buried for about 4000 years, until exposed to view by another storm in 1850. There are ten unroofed, rectangular dwellings interconnected by low covered passages and complete with furniture; food boxes, grinders, beds, dressers − all of stone. There is nothing like it in the whole of Europe.

Five miles away, off the B9055, are the mysterious standing stone circles on lonely moorland between the lochs of Stenness and Harray. The nearby Ring of Brodgar is even more impressive and surrounded by a deep ditch.

A mile to the east on sloping ground near Finstown village is the most awesome chambered tomb in western Europe. Maeshowe is a large grassy mound 24 feet high which was excavated in 1861. The burial cells open off a grand central chamber. When opened, the tombs were found to have been broken into and robbed centuries before by Vikings, who had cut deep inscriptions on the walls. One set dating from 1153 tells that a chieftain and his men took shelter in Maeshowe when snowbound. Two of the party 'lost their wits' which was 'a great hindrance to their journey'.

The full history of the Norse Earldom of Orkney is told in the Orkneyinga Saga. An impressive reminder of that period is the Red Sandstone Cathedral of St Magnus in Kirkwall. It was begun by Earl Rognvald in 1137 and built to the memory of his uncle who was killed in a power struggle. Magnus's remains were not discovered until 1919; they are now sealed in a pillar of the cathedral. The skull had been split by an axe.

Not surprisingly, one often returns from Orkney with a strange feeling of timelessness:

> Like a shuttle the mind shot to-and-fro
> the past and the present, in an instant.

For general information and timetables of travel to, on and between the islands, write to the Orkney Tourist Information Office, Broad Street, Kirkwall, Orkney KW15 1DH. Enclose 50p and an SAE and they will send a variety of leaflets including one on Orkney Birds (10p). For information on RSPB reserves write to RSPB Scottish Office, 17 Regent Terrace, Edinburgh EH7 5BN. Enclose SAE. For general information on Papa Westray, where overnight accommodation is usually required, contact The Manager, Papay Community Co-operative Limited, Beltane House, Papa Westray, Orkney KW17 2BU. Tel: 08574 267. Visits to the island's North Hill reserve should be notified to the Summer Warden, c/o Gowrie, Papa Westray. For the able-bodied only. Warm clothing essential.

Accommodation On Mainland there are hotels in Kirkwall and Stromness. Farmhouse accommodation or self-catering on most islands. Details from the Tourist Office whose comprehensive booklet *Where to stay in Orkney* costs 40p. There is also hostel accommodation for parties. Details from: Education Dept, Council Offices, Kirkwall. Tel: 3538. There is also a Scottish Youth Hostel in Kirkwall, details from: SYH Association, National Office, 7 Glebe Crescent, Stirling FK8 2JA.

CHAPTER THIRTEEN

Shetland

In all, Shetland comprises about 100 islands stretching in a tenuous chain, 70 miles long, between the North Sea and the Atlantic Ocean. Only seventeen are inhabited, the remainder belong solely to the teeming wildlife of birds, seals and Otters. The islands lie closer to the Arctic Circle than to London and on about the same latitude as Anchorage in Alaska, or Leningrad. In every way, Shetland is almost as close to Norway as to Scotland: the first known settlers were Norsemen in the 8th century and the island did not become part of Scotland until 1469. Today the Norse heritage lives on in the culture, place names and daily speech of the Shetlanders.

Not surprisingly, the gale-lashed islands, soaked in salt-spray, are almost treeless; sometimes they are referred to affectionately as 'The Old Rock'. Fortunately, the warm waters of the Gulf Stream ensure surprisingly mild winters and pleasantly cool summers; unlike the Scottish Highlands, insects are not a serious problem. An especial characteristic of Shetland is the seemingly endless twilight of summer nights known as the 'simmer dim'. Blackbirds can be heard singing with a full throat at two o'clock in the morning.

In the 1970s, upon this remote, age-old community of crofters and fishermen, there burst the most formidable invasion since the Vikings stormed ashore twelve centuries ago. North Sea oil technology has in many respects transformed the islands, but fortunately the worst effects of the industry have been concentrated in only a few places. In the north of Shetland Mainland a deepwater inlet, Sullom Voe, has become the main oil terminal and will soon be one of the biggest oil ports in Europe, handling tankers of 300,000 tons. By 1982, two-thirds of Britain's total consumption of oil will flow through Sullom Voe. Since the oil industry came, the population of the islands has increased by 4000 or so to around 21,000.

Inevitably, the repercussions have already transformed Shetland's economic, political and social way of life. There is also no doubt that, sadly, in spite of elaborate safeguards and precautions, the great seabird colonies are now under serious threat. Already there have been oil spillages during handling operations and inevitably there will be more. Above all, hangs the horrifying possibility of a major disaster involving one of the fully laden supertankers.

On the credit side, Shetland has gained splendid new roads and the principal islands are now linked by an excellent passenger/car ferry service. Air communications are also first class. The principal airport is at Sumburgh at the southern tip of Mainland, the largest of the islands. It is advisable to have a car – either brought over on the ferry or hired at the airport. Most of the breeding birds of Shetland can be found somewhere on Mainland. There is wonderful walking with high cliffs and a wilderness of lochs and moorland. In these solitudes Peregrines may be spotted, Whimbrels, divers, skuas, Dunlin and Merlin – to say nothing of the seabirds in their thousands.

The Shetland reserves generally are suitable only for the able bodied, and warm clothing is essential.

Knots on the Dee Estuary during winter (*Heather Angel*)

Guillemots, Kittiwakes and Shags, Inner Farne (*Heather Angel*)

Hermaness, Shetland (*R. J. Tulloch*)

Kittiwakes and Guillemots, Westray, Orkney (*H. E. Axell*)

Loch Garten, Inverness (*Michael W. Richards, RSPB*)

'The Neck', Skomer Island, South West Wales (*H. E. Axell*)

Bempton Cliffs, Yorkshire (*Michael W. Richards, RSPB*)

Heronry at
Northward Hill, Kent
(*Anthony Clay, RSPB*)

Holkham Marshes, Norfolk (*John Mason*)

Hickling Broad, Norfolk (*J. J. Buxton*)

Leighton Moss, Lancashire (*Anthony Clay, RSPB*)

Minsmere, Suffolk (*Eric Hosking*)

Herma Ness National Nature Reserve, Unst. Nature Conservancy Council

In general, the islands hold for birdwatchers an embarrassment of riches, but for sheer spectacle there is nowhere more dramatic than Herma Ness, the most northerly headland in Britain, on the island of Unst. This second largest of Shetland's islands is 10 miles long by 5 miles wide and has the distinction of being the windiest place in Britain – a gust of 177 mph was measured here in 1962.

Herma Ness has now been designated a National Nature Reserve administered by the Nature Conservancy Council. From mid-May to mid-July the 600-foot cliffs become a true bird city with tens of thousands of Puffins, Gannets, Razorbills, Guillemots, Kittiwakes and Fulmars. The nearby moors are the nesting place of the piratical Great and Arctic Skuas. Shetland now has 96 per cent of the British Great Skua population. From the cliff top it is enthralling to watch the aerobatics as the dark brown 'Bonxies', as the Great Skuas are known here, harry the Gannets and other seabirds returning with food for their young. Sometimes, a Bonxie, with its white wing patches showing, will swoop on to a Gannet in full flight, seize one of its great wings and force it to plummet down into the sea and release or disgorge its catch. There seem no limits to the Bonxies' aggressive tactics. For this reason, when walking near one of their colonies it is essential to wear a hat. Persistent dive-bombing attacks may well draw blood from an uncovered pate.

The slightly smaller and more elegant Arctic Skuas are almost equally aggressive. They craftily attack in level flight from behind, which can be even more alarming. There is no recognition problem although some of the Arctics are dark and some light brown; the adults are distinguished by having two central tail feathers projecting spikily beyond the rest of the tail. Arctic Skuas are adept in putting on impressive distraction displays and if you should stray near their nests they trail a wing most dramatically.

In 1972 a rare straggler from the Southern Hemisphere, a Black-browed Albatross, settled forlornly among the Gannets on the point of Saito. Each year it builds a nest on the same ledge half-way down

97

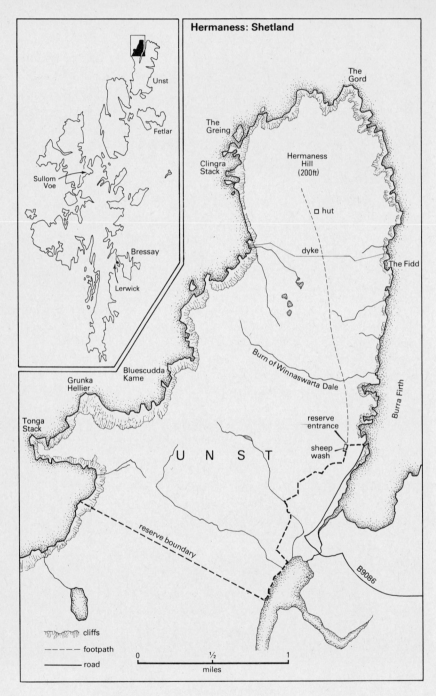

Hermaness: Shetland

Unst

Fetlar

Sullom
Voe

Bressay

Lerwick

The
Gord

The
Greing

Clingra
Stack

Hermaness
Hill
(200ft)

□ hut

dyke

The Fidd

Burn of Winnaswarta Dale

Burra Firth

reserve
entrance

sheep
wash

Grunka
Hellier

Bluescudda
Kame

Tonga
Stack

U N S T

reserve boundary

B9086

cliffs
footpath
road

0   ½   1
miles

the cliff, presumably hoping against hope that another member of the species might one day stray its way.

Apart from seabirds, Unst attracts a greater variety of breeding birds than any other area of comparable size in Shetland. Inland, all the waders on the Shetland list can be found including the Whimbrel, whose trilling call is so characteristic of these remote northern moors. Here too there is a good chance of seeing a Snowy Owl: the remaining three or four females in Shetland now seem to prefer Unst to Fetlar where the first pair bred in 1967.

Almost everywhere you will come across the engaging Shetland Ponies and may well have to slow down your car for a family ambling across the road. They are hard to resist with their shaggy manes, variegated colours and diminutive size – 38 inches is the average height. Wild flowers abound everywhere and there are 400 varieties of plant life.

Access The car ferry landing place is at Belmont in the south of Unst. It is only a short trip from Gutcher on the island of Yell. The drive across Yell will only take about ¾ hour. It is advisable to book the ferry especially in the holiday season. Tel: Burravoe 259. There is also a Loganair service (Monday to Friday) Tel: Gott 246. There are no restrictions to the Herma Ness National Nature Reserve but great care is requested not to cause disturbance to nesting birds.

Accommodation Hagdale Lodge, Britain's most northerly hotel; offers full board. Baltasound Hotel also offers full board; it once had its roof blown off! Apt to be full of oil men. There is also some bed and breakfast accommodation which is mostly excellent. There is a private Youth Hostel at Uyeasound (booking essential); Tel: A. Fraser, Uyeasound 237. A postcard sent from Haroldswick Post Office has an especial frank to show it comes from the most northerly Post Office in Britain.

Stakkaberg Reserve, Fetlar RSPB

Fetlar is one of the islands not to be missed. The name in the Old Norse language meant 'fat land', referring to its fertility. It lies about 4 miles to the south of Unst and to the east of the main north–south chain consisting of Unst, Yell and Mainland. Fetlar is a lush, green island, roughly 5 miles long by 4 miles wide and fortunate in having so far escaped most of the negative features of the oil industry and simply benefited from the advantages.

It first became big news when in 1967 a pair of the magnificent Snowy Owls bred in the rough grass and heather on a hummock, among grazing sheep and ponies. This was the first recorded time that they had bred in Britain and immense interest was aroused. The male Snowy is pure white with a round cat-like face and not much smaller than a Buzzard; the female is slightly larger and her plumage is white speckled with brown. As soon as possible the RSPB warden organized a round-the-clock watch on the nest. The Secretary of State for Scotland granted a Sanctuary Order and the RSPB was then able to establish a 1400-acre reserve. From seven eggs laid, six young hatched and five successfully flew. Their progress was duly reported in the national press, on radio and television. They bred each year on Fetlar until 1975 and, in all, about twenty young were reared. Each spring the old male Snowy usually chased off all the young males. This was also the case in 1975, but then, most unfortunately, he disappeared himself. Since that time, the remaining four or five females seem to spend most of their time on Unst and none of them has been able to find a mate. The Snowies are on the extreme southern edge of their breeding range in Shetland, but the hope is that a young male may one day return to its birthplace or a straggler may appear from Iceland or Scandinavia.

Although the Snowies first made Fetlar a name known to all birdwatchers, the island is also one of the best places in Britain to see whole communities of moorland breeding birds. Many of these species are also at the edge of their range and so the greatest care must be taken to see that they suffer no undue disturbance. The populations of Whimbrel, Red-necked Phalarope and Arctic Tern are of national importance and so the reserve itself is closed during the breeding season. This allows at least a third of the terns and about half the Whimbrel to breed in peace.

The best place to see Red-necked Phalaropes is at their feeding pools in the area of Loch Funzie on the east of the island. There are only about fifty pairs of this exceptionally tame and dainty-looking wader in the whole of Britain and about a quarter of that number can be found on Fetlar in summer.

In spite of its delicate appearance, the bird spends most of its life at sea and migrates to winter quarters off the coast of Arabia and West Africa. There is no more engaging sight than to see a small company of the elegant little birds swimming in a mere, the grey, buff, white and orange of their plumage set off by the vivid yellow of marsh marigolds. Every now and again, they bob their heads and pirouette in small circles to stir up the water insects, which they pick off the surface with their delicate, needle-shaped bills. The most astonishing thing about phalaropes is the sexual role-reversal. The female is slightly larger and more brightly coloured than the male and it is she, a perfect example of the totally emancipated female, who takes the initiative in courtship and in mating. The male is then left to incubate the eggs and also has to tend the young until they are able to fly after seventeen days.

Shetland is also the principal breeding ground in Britain of the Whimbrel, and Fetlar holds about a fifth of the total, which is no more than 100 pairs. This smaller version of the Curlew has two dark stripes on its head separated by a pale streak; the bill is also down-curved but shorter than the Curlew's. The cry is a tittering, quavering sound with a dying cadence and, once heard, never forgotten.

Of other moorland birds there are usually about 60 pairs of Curlew and Golden Plovers, 200 pairs of Snipe, 130 pairs of Lapwings and Oystercatchers and 40 pairs of Ringed Plovers and Redshanks.

Of all the moorland breeding birds, the strange Red-throated Divers are more susceptible to human disturbance than any other species on the island. The greatest care should be taken when observing them. The best places are the Loch of Funzie in the southeast or Papil Water in the west. Here, there are sometimes spectacular displays when new Red-throats arrive from the sea and the resident birds try to scare them away.

These weirdly reptilian birds are a marvel of grace on the water but helpless on land. Their legs, placed well to the rear to give maximum thrust when swimming, are useless for walking. The Red-throats live at sea for most of the year yet prefer to nest by fresh water; they fly up to the moors and seek out small pools which act as landing strips. The two eggs are laid on the ground or on piles of weed only a few feet from the waterside. They are exceptionally handsome birds in breeding plumage when the wine-red throat is set off by the pale grey neck. Their wailing or howling cries must be one of the most melancholy sounds in the bird world.

Photographers should note that it is illegal to visit the nests of Red-throated Diver, Whimbrel, Merlin, Snowy Owl or Red-necked Phalarope without a licence from the Nature Conservancy Council.

Arctic Terns abound on Fetlar and may number more than 4000 pairs. They can be seen at close range, but care should be taken not to walk through a nesting colony as this could result in mass desertion. Like skuas they will dive-bomb intruders fearlessly.

The seabirds are not as numerous as on Unst and there are no Gannets. On the other hand, a night spent on the cliffs at Lambhoga in the south can be exceptionally rewarding. In mid-summer, when there are barely two hours of darkness around midnight, the Manx Shearwaters return from sea to their burrows in the grassy slopes. The night is suddenly full of demoniacal screams and fluttering shapes. Muted sounds can be heard from below ground as the pairs greet each other and change guard over their single white egg below ground. Many little Storm Petrels, black and ghostly and almost impossible to see, nest here too; their white egg is laid deep in a crevice.

The Black Guillemot, or 'Tystie', symbol of the Shetland Bird Club, also breeds here in rock clefts around the coast. Seals can be seen all around the island and Grey Seals breed on northern beaches between East Neap and the Kirn of Gula. There is also a good chance of seeing an Otter at its favourite haunts in the northwest of Fetlar at Brough Lodge and Urie.

Access Car ferry runs three or four times a day from Gutcher on Yell to Oddsta on north coast. Advisable to book in holiday season. Tel: Burravoe 259. Also Loganair service (Monday to Friday) Tel: Gott 246. The RSPB warden should be contacted at Bealance. Tel: Fetlar 246. The reserve is closed during the breeding season.

Accommodation Two guest-houses near Houbie. Some self-catering accommodation.

Noss National Nature Reserve Nature Conservancy Council

This small island offers unforgettable spectacles of 70,000 to 80,000 nesting seabirds. Noss covers only 700 acres and lies just a short boat trip from the east of the island of Bressay, which itself shelters Lerwick harbour. It is therefore easily accessible from Mainland. The island gets its name from the Old Norse word 'Nøs' meaning a nose.

The Noup of Noss rises to nearly 600 feet. It has become a natural grandstand for watching the serried ranks of birds. The sandstone-type rock has weathered into horizontal ledges providing ideal nesting sites. High up on their large untidy nests are 5000 or 6000 pairs of Gannets. Great and Arctic Skuas breed on the high moorland and constantly carry out marauding attacks on the other birds. Eider Ducks surprisingly breed near the skuas and inevitably lose many of their young. Fulmars nest among the cliff-top flowers – sea and red campion, spring squill, sea pink and scurvy grass – on the walk up to the Point of Hovie. On Noss there are incomparable views of all the seabirds and it is one of the best islands for photography.

Access is by car ferry from Lerwick to Bressay: from here the short boat crossing to Noss is subject to weather and tides – check with the local Tourist Information Office.
In summer, visitors should contact the warden at Gungstie House. The walk around the reserve takes 2 to 3 hours: the centre of the island must be avoided in the nesting season. Boat trips around the island are available from Lerwick.
Accommodation None.

Apart from the wild beauty and outstanding natural delights of Shetland it is well worth visiting the capital Lerwick, Britain's most northerly town. The name comes from the Norse 'Leir-vik' meaning clay creek. It still has the feel of a Scandinavian town: grey, uncompromising, salty. Stone houses slope steeply down to the bustling harbour. Visit the Shetland County Museum near the centre of the town. Here there is a fascinating introduction to the Shetland way of life on land or sea.

The islands were undoubtedly inhabited long before the Norsemen came – possibly from at least 2000 BC; and there is no area in Scotland quite so rich in prehistoric remains. Many of the treasures which have been found now rest in Edinburgh, but here there remains a number of priceless relics from Stone, Bronze and Iron Age settlements. There are also splendid examples of Celtic sculptured stones and a wealth of relics from the Viking period.

This may make you wish to visit some of the numerous archaeological sites. One of the best preserved is on the outskirts of Lerwick itself: the substantial remains of an Iron Age broch – a large drystone tower with block houses and living quarters. It stands mysteriously looking out over the south shore of Loch Clickhimin by the main Lerwick–Sumburgh road and incongruously close to a modern housing estate.

Another remarkable site lies close to Sumburgh airport. Among the huge stone walls and jumbled remains of 3000 years of occupation are the ruins of an early-17th-century Laird's house, which Sir Walter Scott featured in his book *The Pirate*, giving it the name Jarlshof. There is another magnificent broch on the little island of Mousa, which also has a good colony of Storm Petrels in summer. It lies opposite Sandwick which is on the Lerwick–Sumburgh road.

The sites mentioned are the most accessible but there is an inexhaustible amount of archaeological interest to be found all over Shetland.

CHAPTER FOURTEEN

Loch Garten Nature Reserve, Inverness

RSPB

There has been no more publicized bird in Britain over the past twenty-five years or so than that spectacular chocolate and white fish-hawk, the Osprey. It fired the imagination of the general public in the spring of 1958, when, after sightings and nesting attempts for a few years previously, a pair finally built an eyrie at the top of a low Scots pine by the side of Loch Garten. The birds had chosen one of the most beautiful parts of the Highlands – the ancient Caledonian Forest of Abernethy in Strathspey, beyond the northern slopes of the Cairngorms. Some of the area retains today a unique, primeval character – much as it must have looked when Wolves and Bears roamed at will.

The RSPB immediately organized a round-the-clock watch on the site, but on the night of 3 June, in spite of all the care, an egg-stealer, somehow, in the dark at 2.30 a.m. managed to climb the 25 feet or so to the nest. The watcher spotted him and, rousing a companion close by, rushed towards the tree but the raider had been able to drop down on to the soft ground, dash into thick cover and escape. Two broken eggs were found at the foot of the tree. An inspection of the nest showed that he had left two hen's eggs, daubed with brown boot polish, in the hope of fooling the RSPB – and the birds.

The following year, the Ospreys returned to a different site on the lochside and completed a nest which they had begun two weeks after the previous year's disaster. Near-military means of security were used by the RSPB including tangles of barbed wire and electronic alarm devices: the precautions paid off and three young were raised. The Osprey had bred successfully in Britain after a lapse of fifty years. Since that spring in 1959, at least forty young Ospreys have flown from the site and now there are some twenty-five other nesting places, most of them secret, in other parts of Scotland. It amounts to a remarkable triumph of nature conservation for the RSPB, the Scottish Wildlife Trust and other conservation bodies.

Nearly a million people have now made the trek to the Loch Garten eyrie and the birds have featured regularly in the national press, and on radio and television. To crown the RSPB's efforts, and as the result of a national appeal, the Society was able in 1975 to purchase the site together with 1500 acres of forest, loch and moorland, to make a magnificent reserve for all time.

The Osprey is indeed a superb bird of prey and here is seen in perfect harmony with its wild surroundings. The wings have a spread of 5 feet or more, the toes are tipped with long, sharp claws curved into a half circle and the pads on the feet have short spines to grip and hold the slippery prey – usually pike or trout. Its dives for fish, feet first, are highly spectacular, but the courtship display is doubly so. After wintering in West Africa, the male usually returns to the eyrie in the first week of April. On a fine day he will then begin his courtship flights. He first circles round and climbs to about 1000 feet; for a moment he will hover; then down he comes in a breathtaking dive. The hen arrives a few days later, observes him it seems admiringly, and the serious business of building up the nest begins. Sticks of all sizes are gathered or broken from trees. The male carries the larger ones, sometimes as much as 5 feet long, in his talons, and always pointing fore and aft. The eyrie itself usually measures about 4 feet across and is very solid as it has to be able to withstand fierce gales. In about the third week of April a clutch of two or three eggs

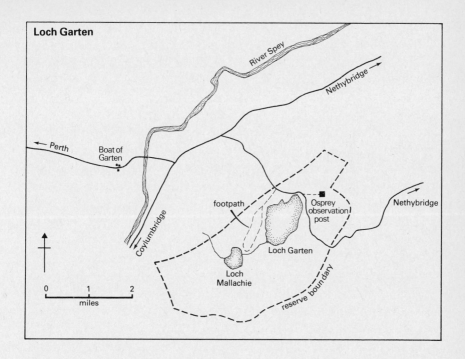

are laid and incubation lasts for thirty-five days. The hen does most of the sitting, while the male forages for fish.

Although the Osprey now seems securely established again in Scotland, the RSPB still arranges constant vigilance during the nesting season at Loch Garten. Nevertheless, in 1977, an egg collector somehow managed to steal the only clutch of four Osprey eggs known to be laid in Britain this century. It is just as well that the maximum fine for egg stealing under the Protection of Birds Act was raised to £500 a few years ago and may soon be doubled.

Loch Garten itself is in the northern part of the Abernethy forest where some of the huge pines are up to 250 years old. In the marshy areas stunted pines and birches provide another important area for wildlife. In all, more than forty species of birds breed in the forest. The most common are Chaffinch, Willow Warbler, Redstart, Crested Tit, Coal Tit, Goldcrest, Meadow Pipit and Siskin. The Crested Tit is fractionally larger than the Coal Tit, which is the smallest of the titmouse family. In Britain it breeds only in the east Scottish

Highlands and, for the most part, in pine woods. Reafforestation is now helping it to move back into other areas from which it had retreated during the time of extensive tree felling in the 17th and 18th centuries. There is no identification problem as the black and white crest is most distinctive and the bird has all the charming ways of the titmice.

Goldcrests are more numerous but can be difficult to see as they are so tiny – $3\frac{1}{2}$ inches, Europe's smallest bird – and keep mainly to the tops of pines. The crests, all golden-yellow in the female, stretch across the crown from front to back and are not usually obvious. In courtship or territorial display, the little quivering male raises his crest and also spreads it sideways to show off a patch of flaming orange.

Crossbills are seen in small numbers in the forest and breed best when the cone crop is abundant. They live almost entirely among the pine cones and have highly specialized bills with the tips crossed to enable them to extract the seeds. Crossbills also feed on larch and Norway spruce. They are among the most colourful of the finch family: the males a fiery crimson, the females yellowish green. Both have dark brown wings and tail and move sideways along the branches like tiny parrots.

Siskins, bright yellow-green with dark streaks, are also colourful members of the same family and breed in the conifers. Until about 1900 they only bred in northern Scotland and the pine plantations of Ireland, but are now setting up colonies in newly afforested areas of England and Wales.

In Abernethy there are also many species from the far north which spend the winter and linger until late spring, before moving back to their breeding grounds. In May, Goldeneyes can sometimes be seen displaying – the drake lays its head back and points its bill at the sky. There may also be a Rough-legged Buzzard or a Great Grey Shrike. In the pools and marshes numbers of Wigeon breed and several pairs of Goosanders nest near lochans on the upper edge of the forest. Two pairs of Long-eared Owls breed at Loch Garten and there are Tawny Owls as well.

By far the largest bird of the pinewood is the cock Capercaillie. This largest of the game-birds became extinct in the British Isles at the end of the 18th century, owing to the felling of pine forests and through persecution. Then in the late 1830s about fifty of the birds were brought from Sweden to a Perthshire estate. They quickly re-established and are now fairly common in the pine forests of the Highlands and even in some parts of the Lowlands too. A cock Capercaillie looks like something from another age, a monster of a black bird about the size of a turkey. In the spring, courtship displays are performed with battles between the males, who strut around and make frequent leaps into the air with tails full spread. These posturings are reinforced with raucous calls, a crescendo of clicks which ends with a loud pop like a cork being drawn from a bottle and then followed by a harsh shriek as of a knife being ground. But to the little brown hen crouching in the heather it is no doubt sweet music and soon there will be a clutch of five to eight eggs which she incubates herself for four weeks in a hollow she has scraped in the forest floor.

Also on the reserve, set among stunted birches and junipers, is the home of the Black Grouse. The polygamous Blackcocks have glossy-black, lyre-shaped tails which are spread in display to show off the startlingly-white undertail coverts. The females are smaller and brownish in colour, but they are always called Greyhens. Their nests are near the edge of the forest, unlike the Red Grouse which nest in the open heather. Among other nesting birds are Curlew, Golden Plover and Wheatear.

Of mammals the most common here are Roe Deer and the native Red Squirrel. Occasionally Otters are seen on the lochs and sometimes in winter there may be a glimpse of a Wildcat or Badger. In all, the Loch Garten reserve holds a unique wildlife community.

As Speyside is now also a booming tourist area, there is considerable pressure on the district and there are increasing demands for all kinds of leisure pursuits. It is clear that the reserve was set up by the RSPB only just in time. Nearby is the Aviemore Centre with every holiday attraction imaginable from winter sports to squash and discos.

Access Via the B970, 8 miles northeast of Aviemore.
Opening times The reserve is open along marked paths all the year round, all

day. The observation hide is open from the beginning of April to the end of August, from 10 a.m. to 6.30 p.m. until early May, thereafter from 10 a.m. to 8.30 p.m.

Facilities Suitable for all the family. The Osprey observation hide is fully equipped and includes information displays.

Warden Tel: Boat of Garten 694.

CHAPTER FIFTEEN

The Farne Islands Nature Reserve, Northumberland

National Trust

A visit to the Farnes is an experience not to be missed. For birdwatchers and equally for lovers of history and unspoilt natural beauty there are rich rewards. This group of small islands lies from about 2 to 6 miles off a remote stretch of the sandy, rock-strewn Northumberland coast; in number they are fifteen to twenty-eight according to the state of the tides. Two of them – the Inner Farne and Staple Island – are open to the public.

Seen from the little holiday resort of Seahouses the islands stretch low and grey against an often misty horizon. Their outlines are wedge-shaped with cliffs to the south and west, sloping away to beaches on the north and east. The islands are an outcrop of black, volcanic rock called dolerite that stretches right across the north of England and is known as the Great Whin Sill.

The Farnes must also be the oldest seabird sanctuary in Europe. St Cuthbert, Northumbria's own saint, lived on the Inner Farne from AD 676 to 684, and then died there three years later in his hermit's cell. He was probably the first person in England to give birds his protection and it was the Eider Ducks that received his especial blessing. He allowed them to nest anywhere they chose, even in his tiny chapel, and nothing was ever allowed to disturb them. In Northumbria today these trusting sea ducks are still known as St Cuthbert's ducks and the saint himself is regarded as the founder of the British conservation movement.

Unfortunately, his example was not always heeded, and with the development of sporting guns in the 19th century a terrible slaughter of seabirds took place. Having proved their marksmanship, the sportsmen were often content to leave the remains of the birds scattered all over the rocky islands. As a result teams of watchers were formed, and their efforts were strengthened by the Bird Protection Act of 1880.

Finally, thanks to a public appeal by Lord Armstrong, patron of the Northumberland and Durham Natural History Society, the Farnes were purchased for the nation in 1925 and handed over to the National Trust. Since then, under an enlightened management, the islands have provided a remarkable object lesson in how to make it possible for wild seabirds to nest in close proximity to thousands of short-staying visitors, including numerous parties of schoolchildren.

The breeding season is from early May to late July, and for sheer spectacle this is the best time of all to visit the Farnes. The motor launch, a converted fishing boat, leaves from the little harbour of Seahouses where Eider drakes gleam black and white as they swim close to the jetty walls.

A short distance to the north across a sandy bay looms the massive, craggy outline of Bamburgh Castle. It soars 150 feet above the sea with battlements spreading $\frac{1}{4}$ mile along the cliff top. From the little village at the foot of the castle Grace Darling, a favourite English heroine, rowed out with her father, the Farnes lighthouse-keeper, on that wild night of 7 September 1838 to rescue nine of the crew from the steamship *Forfarshire*, which had been driven on to the rocks by a gale.

As our boat noses out of Seahouses harbour and points for the islands, small flocks of Guillemots, Puffins and Razorbills pass the bows in quick whirring flight. Overhead, there are Kittiwakes and

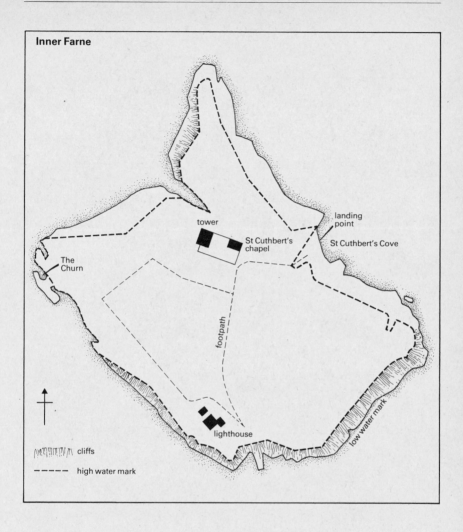

Inner Farne

tower

landing
point

St Cuthbert's
chapel

St Cuthbert's Cove

The
Churn

footpath

low water mark

lighthouse

↑

cliffs

high water mark

gliding Fulmars; Oystercatchers are incessantly piping.

In most years about 20 species nest on the islands with a further
125 or so recorded as visitors. It is above all for the thousands of
nesting terns that the Farnes are famous.

The landing on to the Inner Farne, the largest of the islands
covering 16½ acres, is by rubber dinghy. There is no jetty and so it is
necessary to jump straight on to the seaweed-covered rocks at St
Cuthbert's Cove.

As you walk up the grassy path there are suddenly terns all around and the air rings with their strident cries. These are surely the most elegant of all seabirds with their long pointed wings and deeply forked tails. The nesting birds can be seen closely packed among the sea meadow-grass and white sea campion. The majority are Arctic Terns.

The remarkable thing is that here on the Farnes these shy birds will nest confidently with droves of people walking along paths only a few yards away. These trails are marked only by posts about a foot high: strung between them is a thin rope or wire. The parties of birdwatchers and schoolchildren are usually escorted and the terns, normally so sensitive to disturbance, have become accustomed to the crowds. Even so, at the height of the breeding season, it is advisable to wear a hat. However graceful the birds may appear, they are highly aggressive, swooping down with staccato cries and often pressing home an attack. Even a hat will get thumped but a bald pate will soon, in all probability, be bleeding.

Although smaller and more slender than gulls, they are champion fliers and hold the world record for migration flights. Their breeding range is from Britain to within 700 miles of the North Pole, yet they spend their winters off the coast of South Africa and sometimes even rove as far as the Antarctic pack-ice. In this way, they enjoy more hours of daylight than any other living bird. One Arctic Tern, which lived to a record age of twenty-seven, was reckoned to have flown about 15,000 miles each year on migration – giving it a life total of round about 400,000 miles!

Among the Arctics are smaller numbers of the very similar Common Terns. They have the same glossy black caps but are noticeably paler grey on the body, and, when closely seen, have a black tip to the red bill. Interspersed among the Arctics and Commons, further to test the birdwatcher's abilities, are a very few pairs of the also-similar Roseate Terns. Look first for the whitest-looking of the small terns then try to make out a rosy flush on the breast, note the longer tail and also the black bills which usually have some red at the base. Most distinctive will be the Roseate's harsh 'aark aark' call. The largest of the tern family – the Sandwich – also nests on the Farnes. Apart from their size, they have distinctive black crests and black bills with yellow tips.

Terns are temperamental birds and occasionally, for no apparent reason, a whole colony will take off and fly around in a frenzy, uttering their harsh cries. This is sometimes called a 'dread' of terns. The distinguished artist and naturalist Dr Ennion, who lived near the Farnes, was once asked by a lady visitor what the terns ate. When he replied 'small fish', she looked up at the clouds of screaming wild birds remarking: 'It must cost a hell of a lot to feed 'em.'

The tiny stone chapel dedicated to St Cuthbert was completed in 1370 and restored in the 19th century. It should be entered with care, for within a foot or two of the doorway, a portly, brown-camouflaged Eider is almost certain to be nesting. Incubation lasts about thirty days and she seldom moves. Her handsome black and white mate takes no part. The nest is lined with soft down plucked from her breast and she covers the eggs with it on her rare departures. In some Arctic regions this down is still gathered from the nesting colonies of Eiders and used for quilts.

These sea ducks, which can cope with the ocean in all its fiercest moods, make the softest crooning calls to each other. The sound 'OO – ooo' goes up and down the scale, as though they were expressing astonishment at something mildly shocking. Once heard, it is a sound never forgotten. Most years about 1000 Eiders nest on Inner Farne.

A second ancient stone chapel is used as an information centre; and there is a tower which in the 17th century was used as a lighthouse. A beacon of coal and timber used to be lit each night on its top. This tower is now used as accommodation for the wardens. The modern automated lighthouse is on the cliffs to the south.

This is the highest point on the island, where Kittiwakes, Shags, Guillemots and Fulmars nest on the cliff ledges. Continuing northwest, look out for passage migrants. There may well be a variety of warblers, thrushes and finches; often among them will be an exciting rarity. A list is displayed at the Information Centre in the chapel. Rock Pipits are always present and distinguished from Meadow Pipits by their darker colour and grey outer tail feathers. The main trail then leads to a large pool which is known, with good reason, as the Churn Pool because, in certain conditions, it acts as a blowhole. With a northerly gale, the sea rushes into a cleft in the rock sending a column of water shooting up from the Churn sometimes as high as 90 feet. Here, also, there are splendid views of Holy Island and on the mainland to the north Bamburgh Castle, majestic against a background of the Cheviot Hills.

The path finally turns northeast with views of the red-painted Longstone lighthouse. Oystercatchers and Ringed Plovers nest here in summer and it is a good place to see migrant Turnstones, Dunlins and Purple Sandpipers.

The other island on which the public is allowed to land is Staple Island and on the path down to the boat at St Cuthbert's Cove it can be seen lying about 2 miles to the northeast across Staple Sound.

This is another superb island for seeing birds. Landing straight on to the rocks at the Southeast Hole and following the trail, look out for groups of Puffins gathered on the cliff edges. In this area they are able to nest in burrows honeycombing the peaty soil.

The most astonishing sight of all is provided by the Guillemots. There are at least 1000 crammed together on three stacks of black rock about 50 feet high known as the Pinnacles. Where else in the world can such densely-packed colonies of seabirds be seen at no more than a few yards' range? It is like some extraordinary natural zoo.

The eggs, varying in colour, can be clearly seen on the rock ledges. A Guillemot has only a single egg which it holds awkwardly between its legs, but it might be blue, brown, yellowish or white – some blotched, some not.

At this range, even without binoculars, it can also be seen that some of the Guillemots are bridled. These birds have a slight variation in plumage which makes them appear to be wearing spectacles. A narrow white line runs round the eye and stretches back to the nape. Here on the Farnes only about one in twenty-five birds is bridled.

Close by the Pinnacles is a narrow cleft known as Kittiwake Gully although Guillemots and Shags are now spreading to it too. Here again, at only a few yards' range, are unrivalled opportunities for bird photography. The Kittiwakes, those most engaging, gentle-

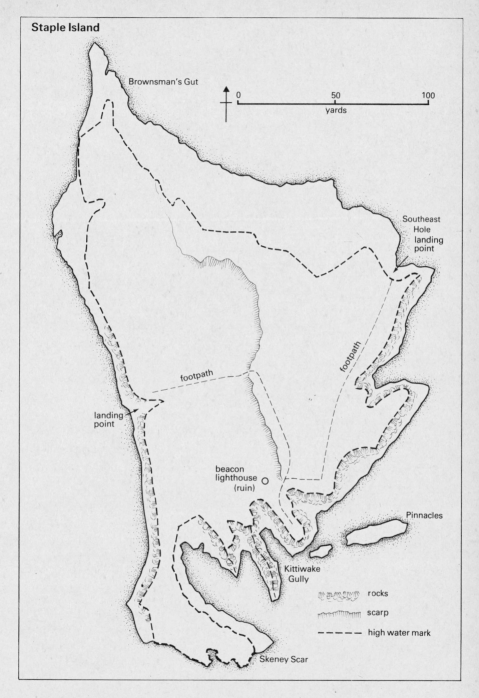

Staple Island

Brownsman's Gut

0   50   100
yards

Southeast
Hole
landing
point

footpath

footpath

landing
point

beacon
lighthouse
(ruin)   O

Pinnacles

Kittiwake
Gully

rocks

scarp

high water mark

Skeney Scar

looking members of the gull family, sit on their untidy cup-shaped nests of seaweed and grass on every suitable ledge where there are no Guillemots, and the air rings with their cries.

Lower down are rocks appearing well white-washed by the reptilian-looking Shags on their large untidy nests. Across the top of the island, among the white of sea campion, are nesting Eiders, the young of which are often prey for Lesser Black-backed and Herring Gulls. Here too are a few Rabbits.

The mammal for which the Farnes are justly famous is the Grey, or Atlantic, Seal. It is larger than the Common Seal and has a distinguished Roman nose. The islands are its only breeding place on Britain's east coast. Staple was once the main island for seals but they are now discouraged there because it was found that when they hauled out to breed in autumn, their heavy concertina-like movements caused serious erosion of the peaty soil and destroyed the sparse vegetation. Burrow-nesting Puffins suffered particularly. Fortunately there are plenty of other suitable breeding grounds for seals on the outer islands. The best time to see them is from October to December, but even in mid-summer they can be spotted on rocky ledges, especially on Crumstone, the most easterly of the islands, and on Longstone to the north. It is always a delight when a retriever-like head with melting eyes bobs up benignly near the boat; yet another magical memory of a visit to the Farnes.

Access By licensed boats from Seahouses Harbour. Trips are subject to weather conditions; check with The National Trust Information Centre, 16 Main Street, Seahouses, Northumberland.

Opening times During the breeding season, from 15 May to 15 July, the two islands are open as follows: Staple Island – 10.30 a.m. to 1.30 p.m., Inner Farne – 2 p.m. to 5 p.m. For the rest of the season the islands are each open from 10 a.m. to 6 p.m. daily. Special permits are available for school parties during the breeding season; apply to The National Trust Information Centre.

Facilities Suitable for all the family. There is an information centre on Inner Farne.

Warden c/o The National Trust, 8 St Aidans, Seahouses, Northumberland NE68 7SR.

CHAPTER SIXTEEN

Bempton Cliffs Reserve, Humberside, North Yorkshire
RSPB

The white cliffs at Bempton on the Yorkshire coast rise sheer 400 feet from the sea; in summer they become a teeming city for upward of 100,000 pairs of seabirds. It is because of all the great breeding colonies around our indented coastline that Britain is of such outstanding importance in the bird world; in this respect we have an international responsibility. Not surprisingly, overseas visitors have sometimes been observed almost dancing a jig on the cliff top at the unforgettable sights and sounds. After all, many populations of seabirds are situated on rocky islands and are often difficult to reach, but here access could scarcely be easier.

The cliffs form the northwest face of the little Flamborough Peninsula which pokes its nose into the North Sea between the holiday resorts of Filey to the north and Bridlington just 4 miles to the south. Bempton even has Britain's only mainland breeding colony of the Gannet. The British Isles now hold three-quarters of the world population of this magnificent seabird with its 6-foot wingspan and ability to catch fish from an aerial dive down to depths of 15 feet. Gannets were first recorded nesting at Bempton in 1937 and have since gradually built up to as many as 270 pairs. In comparison with the tens of thousands to be found on remote islands

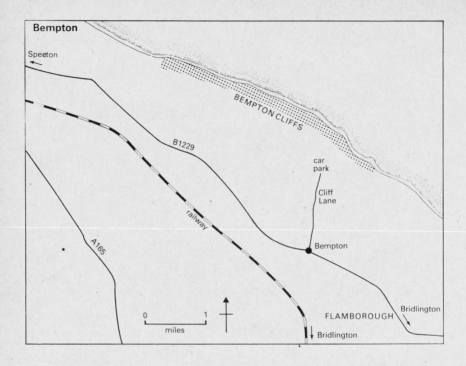

such as St Kilda, Grassholm or the Bass Rock, the number has little significance; the important difference is that here they can be seen with the minimum of effort.

A public path runs the 3-mile length of the reserve, which was established in 1970, and there are excellent observation points giving grandstand views of the cliff-face. On some of the promontories, fences are necessary as the cliffs can be dangerous; but not so long ago these cliffs were also highly dangerous for birds. Bempton is in fact a landmark in the long struggle to set up Britain's bird protection laws, which have now become models for conservationists throughout the world.

The first battles took place here in the 1830s. This was a time when birds, like almost all forms of wildlife, were ruthlessly persecuted for either gain or sport. Not only were the nesting seabirds shot from the top of the cliff, but they also had to face death from the sea. Steamers carrying thirty or so 'sportsmen' used to anchor beneath the cliffs. A resounding hoot from the siren and the frightened birds took off to be confronted with a barrage of shot. They died in their thousands and the young were then left to starve on the cliff ledges.

Local naturalists were appalled by the slaughter and feared that the birds might desert the cliffs entirely. It was only after considerable agitation that the Sea Birds Preservation Act came into being in 1869. This afforded protection for thirty-five scheduled species, at least during the breeding season. It was a start, and progress thereafter continued encouragingly. The setting up of the infant Society for the Protection of Birds in 1889 gave an important fresh impetus; further legislation followed, culminating in the comprehensive Protection of Birds Act of 1954.

This Act also put paid to the activities of the Bempton 'climmers'. These intrepid characters used to be lowered down the cliff-face on ropes to gather the harvest of Guillemot eggs. At one time their haul amounted to 130,000 eggs a year. Some were sold to bakers and confectioners, others were dispatched to Leeds, where the albumen was used to put the shine in patent leather.

It is largely thanks to the protection laws that Britain's total seabird population now stands at about 3 million pairs, and here at Bempton the cliffs hold one of the largest seabird colonies in Britain.

The most numerous species is that small sea-going gull, the Kittiwake; there may well be 67,000 pairs. In the courting season it is their wild chorus – kittee-wayke – which resounds above all the other deafening cries rising from the cliff-face. Except in the breeding season, no other gull is found so often far from land. Like other seabirds, it has evolved so that it can drink sea water and convert it into fresh water within its body. On leaving the narrow ledges on the cliff-face many of the Kittiwakes fly off to the west coast of Greenland where there is a plentiful supply of food. These gentle-looking gulls with their dark eyes, white heads and underparts, grey backs and readily identified by their all-black wing tips, have increased spectacularly since their protection began at the turn of the century. About half a million pairs of these birds now breed around our coasts, many hundreds of them on the window ledges of buildings in ports like Lowestoft where no cliff sites are available.

Of the auk family there are some 8000 pairs of Guillemots packed on long narrow ledges, 1500 pairs of Razorbills in small crevices and about 1000 pairs of Puffins in burrows and holes. The nests of Herring Gulls are widely dispersed but also number about 1000. A hundred years ago that large grey and white member of the petrel family, the Fulmar, used to breed in the British Isles only on remote St Kilda, the most westerly of the Outer Hebrides. Its first recorded nesting on the Yorkshire coast was here at Bempton in 1922; they have now spread to cliffs, and some dunes, in all parts of Britain, though very thinly in the southeast. Like the Kittiwake, the rapid increase of Fulmars is one of this century's most remarkable bird happenings. It may be due to a spreading of warmer seas in the northeast Atlantic or perhaps to an intensified fishing industry discarding large amounts of offal at sea. Bempton now has about 400 pairs.

In all, since the reserve was set up in 1970, 160 species have been recorded and 33 regularly breed. In migration times almost anything is liable to be seen from the cliff-top fields. Up on these windswept heights there are scarcely any trees – just a few hawthorns and crab-apple trees in the low hedges. Of flowering plants, 220 species have been recorded and the most memorable is the glorious expanse of red campion in early summer.

The nearby holiday resort of Bridlington is well worth a visit. Sandy beaches stretch for miles on either side of the busy harbour from which cobles – open-decked fishing boats – run trips. There is also a Priory church. A short distance to the north, in 50 acres of parkland, stands a fine Georgian mansion, Sewerby Hall, which is now owned by the borough. This has an art gallery, a museum and a zoo.

Flamborough has a 14th-century church with a Norman chancel-arch and font. At Flamborough Head itself is the original lighthouse built in 1669. The present one dates from 1806, a stone tower 87 feet high with a light which can be seen for 29 miles. In 1779, just offshore, there was a desperate naval engagement. A small French squadron under the command of the celebrated Scottish-born American, Paul Jones, captured two British men-of-war.

There is much to see in the district and never let it be forgotten that Bempton is also within easy reach of those incomparable Yorkshire moors.

Bempton is just to the east of the A165. A public footpath (open all year) runs along the cliff top from Filey to Flamborough Head. This takes in the 3-mile length of the reserve. The centre of the reserve is reached by driving up Cliff Lane from Bempton village. There is a car park, and a warden (c/o Bempton Post Office, Bridlington, North Humberside) from April to August. Great care must be taken to keep to the footpath and observation points. The cliffs are very dangerous in places. However, the terrain is otherwise suitable for all the family.

CHAPTER SEVENTEEN

The Ouse Washes Reserves

Three conservation bodies have reserves here: The Royal Society for the Protection of Birds, the Cambridgeshire and Isle of Ely Naturalists' Trust (CAMBIENT) and the Wildfowl Trust.

The Ouse Washes are now recognized as one of Europe's most important inland sites for waterfowl: a wildlife haven in the midst of what was once England's Fenland. It took centuries before the Fens became the most scientifically farmed area of Britain as they are today with the Washes forming a vital part of the flood-relief plan. Until only 300 years ago, 1500 square miles of northern East Anglia were just an untamed fastness of endless peat bogs and meres, studded with marshy islands, under the widest of skies. This was the Fenland that defied the Romans and later gave sanctuary to Hereward the Wake against the Normans. Countless thousands of birds bred here and the vast flocks of waterfowl must have been beyond our imagining.

Then, early in the 17th century, Francis, the fourth Earl of Bedford, decided to improve his estates by draining the marshes to provide summer grazing for cattle. He enlisted the help of an experienced Dutch water engineer Cornelius Vermuyden. Vermuyden cut a 20-mile-long dyke in a straight line from Earith in Cambridgeshire to Denver in Norfolk. This became known as the Old Bedford River. It by-passed the meanderings of the Great Ouse and directed the river water more quickly to the sea. Lush grazing meadows soon became the summer scene, but extensive flooding continued in winter. It was twenty years later, owing to the Civil War, before the Dutchman was able to return to cut another big drain parallel to the first, $\frac{1}{2}$mile to the east. This was called the New Bedford River and in between the high banks lay a narrow strip of grassland which served as a flood reservoir, controlled by a complex system of sluices and pumps, and which we know today as the Ouse Washes.

Birdwatchers may dispute as to which is the most exciting time for a visit but, at any season, this remnant of the Fens is a delight for all who love the strange, haunting beauty of the marshes. In all, more than eighty species breed in this sanctuary: a considerable number for an area which is only 19 miles long, $\frac{1}{2}$ mile wide and with very few trees.

Spring sees the nesting of a wide variety of waders, nine species of duck and many smaller birds of the willows, osier beds, sedge and grassland. Then, the drier, though still muddy, conditions of late summer and autumn bring many ground-feeding migrants, especially small waders from the far north, which pause here to build up their strength for the next stage of their annual journey to Africa. But for many people the most dramatic spectacle of all is in mid-winter when the wild swans fly in from their breeding grounds in the remote northern wastes. They are then the star attraction with tens of thousands of ducks as the supporting cast.

Yet, a very different bird first underlined the importance of the area, when in 1952 a pair of Black-tailed Godwits returned to nest after an absence of more than 100 years. For some time the secret was closely guarded in case the birds should be disturbed. Then, in 1964, the RSPB was able to buy sections of the Washes, followed by the Cambridgeshire and Isle of Ely Naturalists' Trust and in 1967 by the Wildfowl Trust. Although once quite common, these splendid-looking waders had ceased to breed in Britain in about 1830 owing to reclamation of the wetlands and intensive shooting. Now, thanks to

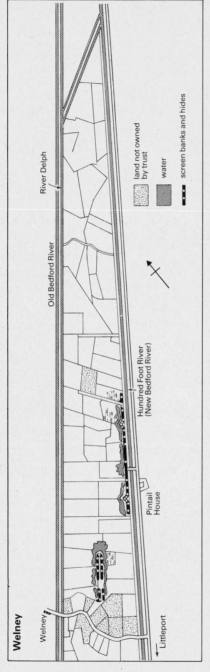

Welney

Welney

River Delph

Old Bedford River

Hundred Foot River
(New Bedford River)

Pintail
House

Littleport

land not owned
by trust

water

screen banks and hides

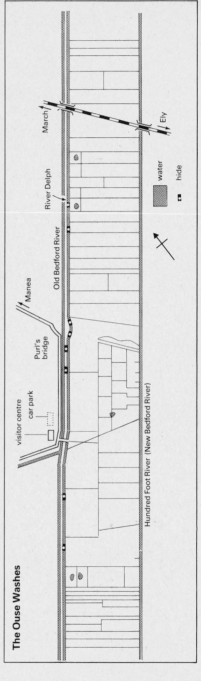

The Ouse Washes

March

Ely

River Delph

Old Bedford River

Manea

Purl's
bridge

visitor centre

car park

Hundred Foot River (New Bedford River)

water

hide

protection and the damp, tussocky meadowland on the Washes these elegant, long-billed and long-legged birds have been able to establish a breeding colony of some fifty-five pairs.

Their return represents a triumph for the three conservation bodies which now control 2700 acres of the Washes. It is certainly a delight to see the Black-tailed Godwits in their summer finery with heads and chests glowing brick-red. A broad black band contrasts with the pure white of the tail, which is often spread out during courtship display flights. The white wing bars are another distinctive feature.

A spring visit may also be rewarded by the spectacle of jousting Ruffs, of which there are now usually between ten and twenty pairs. These extraordinary birds were also once common on the Fens but they ceased breeding in Britain at about the same time as the Godwits and for similar reasons. A Ruff in full breeding splendour is an astonishing sight, with its head set in a flamboyant frill of feathers and backward-pointing ear tufts. The courtship plumes may be black, white, orange, purple or sometimes a mixture of two of these colours. Confrontations are strangely silent and take place on traditional display areas on raised, open ground. The handsome male Ruffs strut around, occasionally tilting at each other, while the smaller and comparatively dowdy females – the Reeves – watch from the sidelines. Finally each Reeve will make her choice, which she indicates by preening the male's frill. Both sexes are promiscuous and the magnificent males play no part whatever in domestic affairs.

A third marshland bird now returning to the sanctuary of the Washes is the Black Tern. This graceful bird, shaped like a large swallow, although plumper, was, like the other two, also once common in East Anglia and on Romney Marsh. In spring and summer the heads of the adult birds are black and the upper parts shade from silver to dark grey, although in autumn and winter, like most other terns, the plumage is grey and white. A distinctive feature is their low, dipping flight over the meres, as they swoop down to pick insect food from the surface of the water. They will also occasionally take minnows and tadpoles. A few pairs have nested irregularly since 1966 and there is also a chance of seeing some on migration between Europe and Africa.

There was further excitement on the Washes in 1975 when for the first known time anywhere in the British Isles a pair of the dainty Little Gulls nested on one of the RSPB's meadows. Unfortunately, a predator killed one of the birds and the eggs did not hatch; but evidently the conditions are suitable and so there is hope that Europe's smallest gull, measuring only 11 inches in length, will eventually make a welcome return here.

Apart from these rarities, the most easily seen and heard of all the birds nesting in the meadows are the Lapwings, Redshanks and Snipe. They abound in their hundreds and all are noisy and spectacular in the breeding season. The Lapwing appears boldly black and white as it performs its brilliant aerobatic displays, uttering the plaintive cries from which it gets one of its alternative names – 'Peewit'.

The Redshank cannot be missed as it flutes and yodels its alarm at anything that moves in its territory. Meantime, the air all around vibrates with that strange wild sound – the drumming of the Snipe. These long-billed, brown and gold birds slice down from on high with tail feathers fanned to produce that reedy, unforgettable sound.

The conditions are of course ideal for ducks: wet grassland, enriched by cattle droppings, the soil softened by annual flooding; there are also plenty of overgrown ponds, ditches and beds of reeds and rushes. Nine species nest on the reserves with Mallards especially numerous. Shovelers average about 150 pairs and there are somewhat smaller numbers of Teal, Gadwall, Tufted Duck, Pochard, Garganey, Shelduck and Pintail.

Conspicuous among the small birds are the Yellow Wagtails – the males darting about among the lush green grass like slivers of gold as they endlessly seek insects for their young. Sometimes one may be seen keeping at bay a huge bullock which has blundered too close to its nest in a tussock. There is no braver sight than the diminutive bird frantically spreading its white-edged tail and hurling defiance.

From mid-September to late March is the time to see the wintering waterfowl. Huge concentrations of duck can be seen from the hides on the high banks, especially when rainfall has been moderate and the sloping meadows are flooded only in parts. There is then a range of feeding conditions from water a few feet deep to grassland no more than damp.

The wet meadows attract vast packs of whistling Wigeon, which can number as many as 35,000. There may also be more than 3000 streamlined Pintails, with a few thousand each of Teal and the other more common species which breed on the Washes. Their numbers are swelled by winter visitors from Scandinavia and Russia. Then, in the deeper waters of the rivers and ditches, there are the diving ducks – among them small numbers of Goosanders and Goldeneye. Short-eared Owls also appear as winter visitors.

The finest spectacle of all is to be found at dusk on the large lagoon excavated in front of the centrally-heated observation building on the Welney Wildfowl Refuge – one of the Wildfowl Trust centres. Access is by a covered footbridge over the 'Hundred Foot' river, so there is no disturbance to the birds. It is a dramatic contrast suddenly to come upon the brilliant scene under floodlights. On the inky waters is a vast company of swans, white and luminous. The night air is full of wild cries, as others wheel overhead after feeding during the day on the black fenlands around; some are perhaps still flying in from their Siberian breeding grounds. As at Slimbridge, the Wildfowl Trust has been wonderfully successful in attracting wintering flocks of Bewick's to the lagoon. The main secret of its success has been the liberal hand-outs of grain along the water's edge and in full view of the large wide windows providing one of Europe's finest wild bird spectacles.

There are astonishingly close views of all three species of British swans flying in and landing with exquisite grace. Others roost and preen. Sometimes over 2000 Bewick's have been concentrated here, representing about one-third of Europe's total. This is also half of all those wintering in the British Isles; most of the remainder will be found at Slimbridge. They are in family parties and it is difficult to believe that the grey cygnets have been strong enough to fly with their parents on the great migration from eastern Russia. They will have triumphed over the worst the weather can do and flown through many a barrage of lead-shot from wildfowlers on the way: a 2000-mile flight of deadly danger at only a few months old is no small achievement. There must be problems in this great concourse on the water in keeping families together. That may explain the considerable amount of neck-bobbing that goes on among the Bewick's, as though constantly signalling to each other.

Among them will be thirty or forty larger swans with necks as straight as walking sticks and having longer bills. These are Whoopers, named after their double-note trumpeting calls. They have a wild, remote look about them and will also have flown from Siberia, some possibly from northern Russia or Iceland. Here too, looking homely with their gracefully curved necks and orange bills, will be ninety or so of the familiar Mute Swans – the males distinguished by a large black knob below the forehead.

To view this great gathering of wild swans at Welney, and in such comfortable conditions, is a privilege and an experience not to be missed. The Trust also owns 800 acres of the water meadows – a refuge for a great concourse of wildfowl.

The Fens, or what remains of them, are a solitary landscape, but many of the small towns are worth a visit. Wisbech on the River Nene is full of history and a splendid row of Georgian houses lends great distinction to the waterfront. The Fenland Museum there has much varied interest including the manuscript of Charles Dickens's *Great Expectations*.

Rising above all, is the city of Ely with its ancient inns, historic houses, shops and alleyways. Its name derives from the Saxon 'Elig' meaning eel island. And an island it was until the Fens were drained in the 17th and 18th centuries. Hereward the Wake sought refuge here and centuries later Oliver Cromwell made it his home for ten years. The Norman Cathedral has a unique, octagonal, lantern tower that was built in 1322 when the original one collapsed. Ely Cathedral is indeed the glory of the Fens.

Facilities for birdwatching in the Ouse Washes reserves are particularly good, and suitable for all the family. The high barrier bank containing the north side of the Washes provides an ideal site for hides. In the western section, between Purl's Bridge and the railway viaduct, the RSPB has built six hides overlooking its property; CAMBIENT have three more on their adjacent reserve. All are free and always open to the public. This accommodation is particularly welcome on a winter's day when Arctic winds can blow across the flat lands and no one should find it necessary to stand in the open on top of the Barrier Bank, thus causing disturbance to the birds.

Access to RSPB and CAMBIENT hides is at Welches Dam where there is a car park and visitor centre. No prior arrangements for visiting are necessary, except that notification of parties of 12 or more should be made to: RSPB Warden, 'Limosa', Welches Dam, Manea, March, Cambs. PE15 0ND.

The Welney Reserve of the Wildfowl Trust is open daily, except Christmas Day, from 10 a.m. to 5 p.m. Unescorted tours include use of the observatory and some 30 small hides. A $\frac{3}{4}$ mile walk leads to a wader area and a scrape.

Escorted tours are available on Saturdays and Sundays and start from the Warden's Headquarters at Pintail House. This is on the road below the Barrier Bank on the south side of the Washes, nearly opposite Welney and $1\frac{1}{4}$ miles from the bridge carrying the A1101 to Littleport. There is a Reception Office and car park. Morning escorted tours are from 10 a.m. to 12.30 p.m. Afternoon tours from 1.45 p.m. to 3.30 p.m. when the wild birds are fed. At the end of either tour visitors may stay on without the warden in new wings of the observatory building. Maximum number for each escorted tour is 50 and advance booking is advisable.

Evening visits for booked parties of 20 or more (members only) are possible from 1 November until 1 March. They begin at 7 p.m. and last for about 1 hour and afford splendid views of swans by floodlight. A leaflet giving charges and other information is available on application. Highly recommended for viewing in comfort.

For a limited number of visitors wishing to see both the morning and evening flights, simple overnight accommodation of bed/bunk and breakfast is available at Wigeon House, next to Pintail House.

For further information contact The Warden, Pintail House, Hundred Foot Bank, Welney, Wisbech, Cambs. Tel: Ely 860711.

CHAPTER EIGHTEEN

The Coast of North Norfolk

This is one of the most varied and fascinating coastlines in England for birdlife, scenic contrast and historical association. Along a 35-mile stretch from Snettisham on the Wash, northward and round the chalk-cliffs at Hunstanton, then eastward along the shallow edge of the North Sea to Weybourne lie no fewer than ten bird reserves. That is an indication of the variety of scene, with sea, sky and mud as the chief ingredients. In addition, there are sand dunes, shingle banks, spits, saltings, vast intertidal flats, freshwater marshes, ponds, pine woods and isolated copses. Much of the shore just belongs to the birds and the sea.

The North Sea is one of the roughest and most unpredictable expanses of water in the world and the Norfolk coast receives the full brunt of it unchecked from the Arctic. Not surprisingly, the coastline is forever changing, especially when surges built up by northwester-lies coincide with spring tides. Wave, wind and tide dictate the way of life: the crab-boats and yachts just sail when they can.

Fortunately, the main road, the A149, does not hug the coast and the reserves lie between it and the sea. They are reached down byways from a number of boulder and sandstone villages – ancient settlements from Saxon times, with their flint-towered churches ensconced in trees.

First, a general look at the whole area. This northwest corner is known as Royal Norfolk, and a good place to begin the visit would be by way of King's Lynn, which has been a prosperous port since medieval times when it was called Bishop's Lynn. Henry VIII changed its name and the town was later to become a royalist stronghold, suffering siege by Cromwell's troops. Here, there is history all around you. A Lynn man, William Clabourne, became Virginia's first Secretary of State; and George Vancouver gave his name to the island 5000 miles away, after navigating the north coast of western America in 1790. It needs considerable strength of mind to part from all Lynn's character and charm.

Take the road north, which is well wooded and undulating, and soon you come to Castle Rising – a deeply moated Norman keep – still standing square, broad and dominant. Continue north for a mile or two and there is another royal demesne, in total contrast, Sandringham House, the Queen's country home. A 19th-century house bought by Edward VII, set among rolling acres of heath and woodland. Long, straight roads bisect the 7000 acre estate; in summer there is no better place for a family picnic. A few more miles along the road lies the little village of Snettisham with access to the RSPB reserve, which we shall be visiting later. Next, Caley Mill and, if it is July, the fields are misty blue and all around is the scent of lavender.

At the modern holiday resort of Hunstanton overlooking the Wash, an east coast town facing west, the chalk and red-rock cliffs rise to 50 feet; the road curves to the right past wide sands and marshes until, after 7 miles, the tiny village of Titchwell appears with its round-towered church of flint and stone. Here too there is another RSPB reserve.

A short distance further along the coast are the National Trust reserves of Brancaster with the mile-wide strip of saltings, and the offshore island of Scolt Head. A clutch of eight Burnhams come next; they are all a delight. Burnham Thorpe lies just inland and has the distinction of being the birthplace of Admiral Lord Nelson, who was born in the rectory there in 1758.

Back on the coast road continuing east is Holkham Hall, one of England's great 18th-century mansions built on reclaimed dunes and saltmarshes. On a lake in the well-timbered park are numerous wildfowl and a large flock of Canada Geese. The road then takes us through Wells-next-the-Sea and the villages of Stiffkey and Morston. Blakeney and Cley were flourishing ports in medieval times, but their harbours silted up long ago, and their fame today lies with yachtsmen, wildfowlers and birdwatchers.

Now we take a closer look at the whole area which we can regard as one great bird reserve. In general, the terrain and facilities here are suitable for all the family.

Cley Marshes Nature Reserve Norfolk Naturalists' Trust

If there were only time to visit one of these reserves then Cley (pronounced 'Cly' as in Clyde, and lorded over by a fine eighteenth-century windmill) it would have to be. There is magic in the name for birdwatchers and it was here when wildlife was under dire threat from punt-gunners, shooting syndicates and egg collectors that a great conservation movement got under way. The prime mover was Dr Sydney Long, a distinguished naturalist who in March 1926 with a few friends outbid a syndicate when 400 acres of marsh came up for sale. Shortly afterwards, the Norfolk Naturalists' Trust was formed, the first important move to organize conservation on a county basis. Norfolk pointed the way for all the County Trusts throughout Britain.

At Cley, across a strip of marsh giving access from the coast road to the sea, is a $\frac{3}{4}$-mile-long embankment – the East Bank – which has become hallowed ground for birdwatchers in search of rarities. This bank forms the eastern boundary of the reserve and gives splendid views of a wader pool and of wildfowl on the more distant Salthouse marshes.

There are also reed-beds with some breeding Bearded Tits, a few

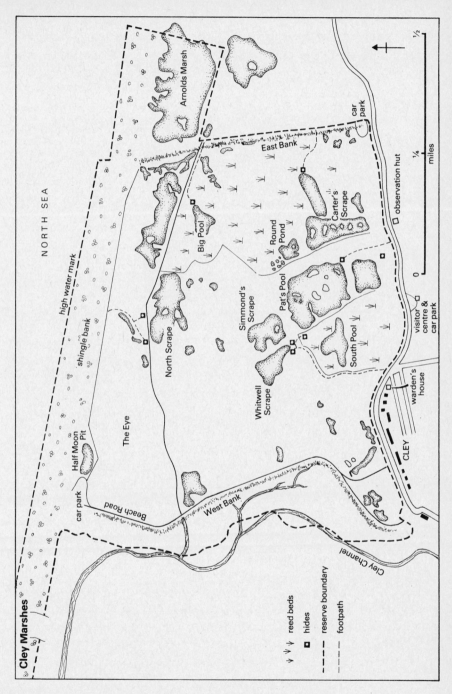

Cley Marshes

NORTH SEA

Arnolds Marsh

car park

East Bank

observation hut

Carter's Scrape

Big Pool

Round Pond

Simmond's Scrape

Pat's Pool

North Scrape

South Pool

visitor centre & car park

Whitwell Scrape

warden's house

CLEY

high water mark

shingle bank

The Eye

Half Moon Pit

car park

Beach Road

West Bank

Cley Channel

½

¼

miles

0

reed beds

hides

reserve boundary

footpath

pairs of Bitterns and Black-tailed Godwits in the tussocky fields. A recently constructed 'scrape' on the Minsmere pattern with shallow lagoons and nesting islands has triumphantly brought the return of Avocets to Cley after an absence of 150 years. Among the many other breeding birds are Water Rails, Yellow Wagtails, Reed and Sedge Warblers and Reed Buntings.

One of the main reasons why the North Norfolk coast is so attractive for birdwatchers can be seen from the map. In autumn, warblers and many other birds, migrating by night from the Baltic area and Scandinavia to winter quarters in the south, often fly into storms and headwinds; they then gratefully make a landfall along this stretch of coastline that bulges out into the North Sea. On some mornings, thousands of exhausted birds can be seen searching the maritime grasses and shrubs for insects or seeds. In October and November the thick hedgerows of hawthorn are alive with Fieldfares, Blackbirds and Redwings gorging themselves on the red berries.

Flocks of sea ducks, waders and gulls may be seen flying offshore or feeding and resting in the shallows at low-tide. Terns are often harried in flight by piratical skuas, which dive-bomb the unfortunate birds until they disgorge in the air; the skuas then swoop down to gobble up a free meal.

The whole coastline is particularly good for birds in winter and has produced many first sightings for the British list. Here at Cley little parties of Shore Larks with their distinctive black and yellow markings on face and breast can be seen along the high shingle ridge. They have two black tufts, or horns, in breeding plumage and in Britain, where many spend the winter, they are seen shuffling about among the stones and sparse vegetation. They are often in the company of Snow Buntings, which appear mainly brown when seen on the ground, but show a flicker of white wings when they are flushed and there is something of the butterfly in their pattern of flight. In all some 300 species of bird have been recorded at Cley.

Access Via the A149 just east of Cley. There is a car park near the visitors' reception centre on the main road. Cars should not be parked on the narrow coast road, which is often congested at holiday-time.

Opening times From the beginning of April to the end of October daily except Mondays.
Permits Available on site. The East Bank path and foreshore are public.
Facilities There is an observation hut (accessible to the disabled) and eight hides on dry paths through the marshes; a public hide is also available near the reserve.
Warden Watchers Cottage, Cley, Holt, Norfolk.

There remain nine other reserves on this splendid stretch of coast. As Cley is the most easterly, here are the remainder, in sequence, heading west along the A149.

Blakeney Point Nature Reserve National Trust

This 5-mile-long spit of shingle piled up by the sea blocked Blakeney as a port, but has now established it as a favoured holiday-place for small-boat sailors, artists, naturalists and above all birdwatchers. It became Norfolk's first publicly owned reserve when it was bought for the National Trust in 1912. Over the years, low sand dunes formed on the ridge with sparse cover from plants like sea sandwort, sea lavender and thrift. Lying in the path of migrant birds, this is one of the best places to see rare species: Bluethroats and Barred Warblers are regular visitors in August and September.

Among the breeding birds there are good numbers of Common Terns, Shelducks, Oystercatchers and Ringed Plovers. The rare Little Terns nest in increasingly encouraging numbers; Sandwich Terns occasionally breed here and can always be seen in spring and summer. Sea watching is excellent but it should be remembered that the Point is a long way from shelter.

The Point can be reached from Cley by walking west for 5 miles along the shingle bank. It can also be reached by boat about 2 hours before or after high-tide. Enquiries should be made from the local boatmen. Warden: National Trust, Blakeney Point, Morston, Holt, Norfolk. Tel: Cley 480.

Morston Marshes National Trust

These 550 acres of saltings and tidal creeks lie at the south side of Blakeney Harbour on the old estuary of the River Glaven. As everywhere along this coast, there is interest for birdwatchers and botanists. Access is by public footpaths from Blakeney and from Morston Quay.

Holkham National Nature Reserve Nature Conservancy Council

This is the largest of the string of Norfolk coastal reserves. It covers 4250 acres of the Earl of Leicester's estate with another 5500 acres of intertidal sand and mud leased from the Crown Estate Commissioners.

After a visit to the lavish magnificence of the Hall, there is great interest for the birdwatcher, thanks to the profuse planting of conifers, mostly Corsican Pines. They form a wind-break along the entire extent of Holkham's frontage to the sea. This has helped transform what to all but naturalists were once barren sandy wastes into rich and fertile ground. A variety of woodland birds can be seen from the public paths and sometimes migrant Firecrests and Crossbills. On the lake in the grounds there are large flocks of free-flying Canada, Egyptian and Greylag Geese, swans and many other waterfowl.

One reaches the reserve on foot from the car park at Holkham Gap or along the sea wall from Overy Staithe and Wells beach (car park near the quayside). There are good public footpaths leading across the reserve. Warden: 'The Hips', Station Road, Burnham Market, Norfolk. Holkham Hall is nearby.

Brancaster National Trust

This was once part of the Manor of Brancaster and consists mainly of foreshore, sand dunes, reclaimed marshland and saltmarshes. There is considerable wildlife interest.

Access is from the public car park at north end of the beach road from Brancaster village. Warden: 'Corner Cottage', Thornham, Norfolk.

Scolt Head Island National Trust/Nature Conservancy Council/Norfolk Naturalists' Trust

This excellent shingle-beach reserve runs for $3\frac{1}{2}$ miles between Burnham Overy and Brancaster harbours. It is most notable for its nesting colony of a few thousand pairs of Sandwich Terns. This is the largest and whitest of our terns and has a black bill. Their nests are closely packed and in hot, still weather there is quite a stench from the birds' droppings and the remains of uneaten sand-eels.

The island can be visited by arrangement with boatmen from Brancaster Staithe. At no time is it advisable to walk to the island across the tidal saltings. The ternery may not be entered during May to July. There is a nature trail – explanatory leaflet available from the Warden, Dial House, Brancaster Staithe, Norfolk.

Titchwell Marsh Reserve RSPB

A small reserve of 420 acres yet, thanks to a variety of habitats, a wide range of birds may be seen at any time of year. Access is by public footpaths from the coast road between Thornham and Brancaster. There is a public hide on the sea wall.

Holme Dunes Nature Reserve Norfolk Naturalists' Trust

This is another reserve with varied interest. Dense thickets of silvery-green sea buckthorn with orange berries and the dark purple fruit of sloe attract many migrants. The reserve has a reputation for producing rare sightings.

The reserve is reached by car from Holme village – turn right before the beach down the private road leading to the warden's house (car park) – or on foot from Thornham west along the sea wall. It is open every day except Tuesdays between 10 a.m. and 5 p.m.

Permits are required but these are available on site from the warden. There are two hides on the reserve and a visitors' room at the warden's house. The foreshore is accessible to the public throughout the year. Warden: 'The Firs', Holme-next-the-Sea, Norfolk.

Holme Bird Observatory Norfolk Ornithologists' Association

Like the reserve, the observatory is strategically situated on a right-angled bend at the northeast corner of the Wash. Gibraltar Point is 12 miles across the water on the opposite corner. There are traps and nets for catching and ringing migrants; rarities may be seen, especially in autumn.

Access is as for the Holme Dunes Reserve but the observatory is open all year daily (except Tuesdays) from 11 a.m. to 4 p.m.; permits are required but are available on arrival. There are four hides and a ringing room. Warden: 'Aslack Way', Holme-next-the-Sea, Norfolk.

Snettisham Reserve RSPB

This is the tenth reserve on the North Norfolk coast and is situated on the eastern shore of the Wash. It consists of 140 acres of shingle ridges and flooded gravel pits bought by the Society in 1972 together with 3000 acres of intertidal saltings and mudflats leased from the Crown Estate Commissioners.

An unusual feature is that lumps of broken concrete, once part of a road laid for gravel extraction which was destroyed by the great flood of 1953, now benefit breeding birds. With the addition of shingle, they have become nesting islands for Common Terns; and holes between the jagged blocks are used by a few pairs of Wheatears and many Shelducks.

South of the shingle banks on the saltings there is an important feeding and roosting site for waders which use the Wash as a staging post on their journeyings between the Arctic breeding grounds and winter quarters in Britain and Africa. In winter there may be as many as 40,000. There are also large numbers of wildfowl including a flock of Pink-footed Geese. Sometimes 100 or more Little Grebes compete with diving ducks in feeding on sticklebacks in the pits. Occasional visitors including Snow Buntings, Little Gulls, Skuas, Shore Larks and Great Grey Shrikes add to the interest.

To reach the reserve turn off the A149 to the public car park at Snettisham Beach; access is also by footpath from Dersingham. There are three public hides. Warden: Old School Cottage, Wolferton, King's Lynn, Norfolk.

CHAPTER NINETEEN

Hickling Broad
National Nature Reserve, Norfolk
Norfolk Naturalists' Trust/Nature Conservancy Council

How astonished the peat-diggers of medieval times would be to see the host of carefree holidaymakers afloat today on that great complex of waterways, the Norfolk Broads. The huge, shallow pits they dug were flooded by nearby rivers in the late Middle Ages, and Broadland with its peculiar charm and character gradually came into being.

It is formed around three gently tidal rivers: Waveney in the south, Yare in the middle and Bure in the north. Water and land seem to merge in this elusive area of reed-fringed rivers and shallow lakes, interspersed with farms and villages. Above all, there is the widest of skies and a remarkable clarity of light.

So popular have the thirty or so Broads now become that, inevitably, there is pollution and disturbance from the thousands of cabin-cruisers in use each summer. Even greater harm to wildlife is caused by the effluent from about thirty sewage treatment works in the neighbourhood.

Mercifully, all is not lost; there are several reserves which provide much needed sanctuary. The most significant is here at Hickling, the largest of the Broads. Only 3 miles from the sea, it connects with the River Thurne, a tributary of the Bure, and extends over 1360 acres of which nearly one-third is the Broad. It was partly bought and partly leased by the Norfolk Naturalists' Trust in 1945 and with the help of the Nature Conservancy Council was designated a National Nature Reserve in 1958.

Norfolk has produced a long line of great sportsmen-naturalists going back to John Caius in the 16th century. In this tradition, Lord Desborough first made a breeding sanctuary of his Hickling estate after the First World War, when marshland birds had become scarce because of the drainage of wetlands for agriculture and through out-of-season shooting.

The concern for conservation had already brought about the return of that strange bird the Bittern, which Jim Vincent, Hickling's gamekeeper-naturalist, and Miss Emma Turner, one of the first bird photographers, found nesting again at Sutton Broad in 1911. The bird had stopped breeding in Britain by 1868, so its return was hailed as a considerable triumph. Unfortunately, owing to pollution, only a few pairs remain at Hickling today. Bitterns are difficult to see as they skulk in the reed-beds. Their plumage is a blend of brown and cream, a perfect camouflage, as with neck and dagger-like bill pointed to the sky, they merge indistinguishably with the reeds. Their long green toes enable them to move over the softest mud and, by grasping a bunch of reeds with each foot in turn, they can pass through the beds at different levels. The Bittern is more often heard than seen. Indeed, the birds are often invisible to each other, which is no doubt why they developed a call that in tone and penetration resembles a distant fog-horn. The sound can carry up to 3 miles and is usually repeated three to five times. The boom of the Bittern holds the very spirit of the lonely marsh and must be one of the strangest sounds in the world of birds. In 1915, four years after the return of the Bittern, the Marsh Harrier with its characteristic reed-top glide again became a regular nester in Broadland. Both species may be seen at Hickling today but their situation remains precarious.

Considerable scientific investigation goes on to combat pollution and to try to save the threatened ecology of the Broads. Fortunately, Hickling is very shallow and soft-bottomed, so holiday-craft keep mainly to a marked, 6-foot-deep channel, where Coots, Moorhens,

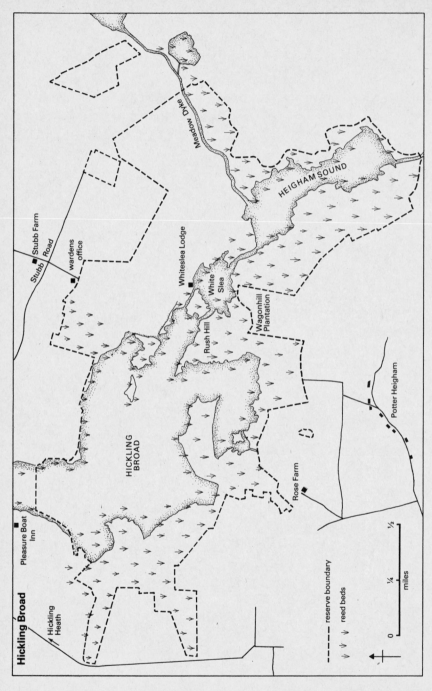

Hickling Broad

Mute Swans and Mallards come right alongside to take food, which pleases the photographers.

For the successful management of the reserve, water levels in the different enclosed sections are carefully maintained by pumps and sluices. At intervals in rotation, the reeds are cut in winter for thatching and the saw sedge cut in summer, so that areas of standing plants and stubble benefit birds in different years. Some water plants have been reduced by Coypus, the aquatic mammals brought to Norfolk from South America in 1929 for the fur trade. In 1937 a few escaped and they multiplied exceedingly as they can have two or three litters a year of three to eleven young. They look something like monster rats except that they have blunt noses, long orange-coloured incisor teeth, webbed hind feet and scaly tails. Another extraordinary feature is that the females have teats high along their sides; the young often cling to these when the mothers are swimming and they can then be seen being dragged along the surface. Coypus are now widespread in the waterways of Norfolk and Suffolk. Nevertheless, the greatest cause of loss of water plants on the reserve is due to reduced water quality, resulting from agricultural drainage water and droppings from the high population of roosting Black-headed Gulls.

The area from Hickling to Horsey has few trees as a result of the flooding in 1939, when the sea breached the coastal dunes. The fen is now more open and milk parsley has spread. This is the main food of the caterpillars of Britain's largest butterflies – the Swallowtails – and these elegant beauties can be seen in May and June making their strong, flapping flights over the reeds. This area is one of their last sanctuaries.

Alders and willows grow thinly along the sides of ditches and channels and there is a large stand of much older trees – Wagonhill Plantation – with some splendid oaks. In the middle of this wood is a 50-foot-high observation tower which gives excellent views of Broadland.

Another feature at Hickling are the artificially created 'scrapes' with hides giving good views of a wide variety of waders, especially migrant sandpipers and 'shanks' on the mud, mown grass and shallow water. On the Broad there are Great Crested and Little

Grebes and several species of duck including Gadwall and Garganey.

The reserve has seven hides, three of which can only be reached by boat. One of these overlooks a partly scraped area where, remarkably, a new colony of Little Terns has established itself – nesting on the bare earth or short mown grass. They normally breed on sand and shingle beaches but have suffered greatly in their normal habitats from the inevitable disturbance by holidaymakers. There are also a few Common Terns and rarities such as Black Terns and Spoonbills frequently visit the reserve in spring and summer, as do many plovers, Ruffs and other waders.

The most important of the small birds dependent upon reed-bed management is the Bearded Tit, a resident and partially migrant species. Reed, Sedge and Grasshopper Warblers are common in summer and fair numbers of Reed Buntings are present throughout the year. A much newer resident, which has extended its range from southern Europe, is Cetti's Warbler, but it is still very rare and difficult to see as it skulks among the reeds and waterside brambles. It is more likely to be spotted by its distinctive, explosive song, reminiscent of the opening bars of Maurice Chevalier's 'Valentine'. Grunts and pig-like squeals are sometimes heard as Water Rails move furtively among the reeds and rushes that in summer are bright with purple and yellow loosestrifes, marsh bedstraw, great water dock and many other plants.

These varied habitats enable eighty species to nest on the reserve and also attract a large number and variety of passage migrants. Hickling has long been famous for its wintering waterfowl and it is well worth visiting the nearby 'Royal Shooting Lodge' at Whiteslea which was much favoured by King George V. It is built almost in the water, beautifully thatched and has a distinctive period atmosphere.

Hickling has the added advantage of being only 25 miles from the fine old city of Norwich, which deserves to be visited for a hundred reasons, but especially for its ancient castle, glorious Norman cathedral and one of the finest museums in England.

Access Off the A149 to Hickling Green then take Stubb Road from the Greyhound Inn. There is a car park by the warden's office.

Opening times From the beginning of April to the end of October daily except Tuesdays from 9.30 a.m. to 6 p.m.

Permits Half-day permits only; apply in advance to Hickling Broad National Nature Reserve, Warden's Office, Stubb Road, Hickling, Norwich NR12 0BW. Tel: Hickling 276.

Facilities Suitable for all the family. Tours including a boat trip and visits to seven hides (tours A & B, available Sunday mornings and all day Mondays, Fridays and Saturdays) or without boat trip and visiting only four hides (C & D, available whenever reserve is open except between 1st November and 31st March when they are available only by special arrangement and at the discretion of the Warden). Special 2½-hour 'Water Trail' tour: boats leave from the Pleasure Boat Inn, Staithe, at 10 a.m. and 2 p.m. There is also a Water Trail operating on Tuesdays, Wednesdays and Thursdays from the end of May to the end of July; thereafter to mid-September, daily from Monday to Friday. It, too, runs from the Pleasure Boat Inn. Picnics may be taken in the hides; there is a shop at the main entrance.

Other sites in the area:

Bure Marshes National Nature Reserve Nature Conservancy Council

This is a very important wetland reserve of 1019 acres, including Hoveton Great Broad (nature trail available May to September daily except Saturdays), Hoveton Little Broad, Ranworth Broad, Cockshoot Broad and Woodbastwick Fen. Many notable plants to be found here include royal fern, marsh fern and water soldier. Milk parsley is common, to the benefit of the Swallowtail butterfly, which is the subject of propagation studies by Nature Conservancy Council scientists who carry out many other investigations here. Breeding birds include Common Terns nesting on rafts, Garganey, Gadwall, feral Egyptian and Canada Geese, Lesser and Greater Spotted Woodpeckers, Woodcock, Water Rail, Bearded Tit and various warblers. Passage birds include Osprey, Black Tern and Pochard. Grey Herons nest nearby and there is a notably large roost of Cormorants.

The reserve is reached via Woodbastwick off the B1140 Norwich to Acle road. Permits are required; apply in advance to The Nature Conservancy Council, 60 Bracondale, Norwich, who will also provide details of opening times and of the nature trail (guide booklet 5p.).

Breydon Water Local Nature Reserve Norfolk County, Suffolk County and Great Yarmouth Borough Council Management Committee

The reserve covers about 4 square miles of mudflats and tidal waters in the estuary of the Rivers Yare and Waveney on the northwest side of Great Yarmouth. It is notable for its wide variety of migrant and wintering waterfowl and waders. Also visiting are Hen and Marsh Harriers, Short-eared Owls and other birds of prey and many finches and buntings. Spoonbills and Black Terns may occur in summer. Birdwatching is good throughout the year. Public footpaths on each side of the estuary reach from Great Yarmouth via the Haven Bridge (for the south side) or the Vauxhall Bridge (for the north side) to the Roman fort at Burgh Castle.

Horsey Mere National Trust

The reserve's 120 acres of open water and reed-beds attract a similar range of marshland birds to that of Hickling Broad but fewer waders. Black Terns occur in Summer, Marsh Harriers are present during the year and Hen Harriers, Short-eared Owls and other raptors are seen from autumn to spring. Nearness of 1 mile to the sea results in more small migrant birds being seen, and shrubs in the coastal dunes are especially worthy of attention. A public path starts from Horsey Mill, which is a landmark alongside the B1159 coast road, 10 miles north of Great Yarmouth.

CHAPTER TWENTY

Minsmere Nature Reserve, Suffolk
RSPB

Minsmere – a name to conjure with in the bird world. Evocative of the lonely marsh, it lies behind the dunes not far from Britain's most easterly point; Holland is just 100 miles across the North Sea. In mid-summer, sky and sea merge in a haze of smoky-blue; the light is soft yet luminously clear, seductive to landscape painters. This is a part of Suffolk's Heritage Coast that stretches from Kessingland down to the Essex border. Happily, there is no coastal road so, for the most part, few people; to a large extent the area belongs to the birds.

Roughly half-way along is Minsmere. Two miles to the north, the ruins of an ancient priory, poised on a crumbling cliff top, are all that remains of the lost city and port of Dunwich, its nine churches swallowed up by the sea. Legend has it that on stormy nights bells can still be heard tolling beneath the waters. The same distance south and there is a discordant note; the biscuit-box outlines of the nuclear power station at the tiny hamlet of Sizewell. At least, it has been proved here that technology and conservation, given the will, can exist in harmony side by side.

The 1500 acres of the reserve attract a wider range of birdlife than any other area in Britain of comparable size: each year, 100 species breed here and some 210 are recorded. It is generally considered to be not only the finest of the RSPB reserves but also one of the best in Europe. The main reasons for this are, first, the remarkable variety of habitats – sand dunes, reed-beds, meres, woods, heath and arable land, grazing marsh and scrub – then, thanks to its position, it offers a safe landfall and resting place for tens of thousands of birds on their vast twice-yearly movements between Africa and northwest Europe and, in addition, the reserve has won world-wide fame for the pioneering of new conservation and marshland management techniques.

Notable among them is the jewel in Minsmere's crown, known as the 'Scrape'. In what was an unproductive, mainly dry area of tangled couch grass which supported only some forty pairs of birds of six species, lagoons of brackish water have been shallowly excavated by machines and hand tools. Many islands were then constructed, with varying surfaces, to meet the specialized nesting and feeding requirements of several threatened species. The depth and salinity of the water is controlled by sluices so as to provide a living soup for birds – tiny shrimps, worms, snails and insects. As a result, 1500 pairs of more than twenty species have been added to the reserve and, most important among them, the Avocets and Little Terns. In addition, a great variety of migrant waders rest and feed here each spring and autumn. These include various plovers, sandpipers and stints, Black and Bar-tailed Godwits, Spotted Redshanks, Ruffs and always a few rarities. A few Spoonbills may stay from late spring to early summer, when a Purple Heron can often be seen or an Osprey may drop in to fish. Spotted Crakes are rare in both seasons but have occasionally bred. Ring Ouzels and Wrynecks are also seen from time to time. Excellent views of these and dozens of other waders, seabirds and waterfowl can be had from spacious hides on the well-screened paths around the Scrape. Many of these have easy access and viewing facilities for disabled persons.

Another aspect of Minsmere's importance is that it forms a vital link in a chain of reserves for many of northwest Europe's birds whose specialized habitats are fast disappearing. Wetlands in particular are being lost through drainage and land reclamation; the new marsh developed here was therefore doubly welcome. The odd

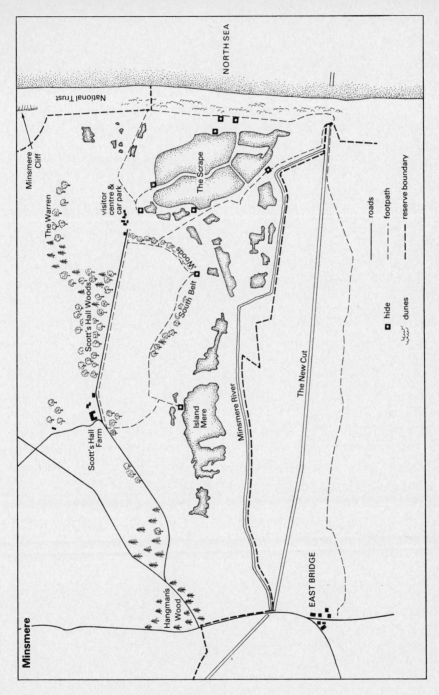

Minsmere

NORTH SEA

National Trust

Minsmere Cliff

The Warren

The Scrape

visitor centre & car park

Scott's Hall Woods

Woods

South Belt

Scott's Hall Farm

Island Mere

Minsmere River

The New Cut

Hangman's Wood

EAST BRIDGE

roads
footpath
reserve boundary

hide
dunes

thing is that it only came about by accident. During the last war, a low-lying area, once the tidal estuary of the little Minsmere River, was flooded as a coastal defence measure. When the sluices began operating again, a large expanse of reed-beds and shallow meres had come into being. The RSPB was quick to realize its importance when four pairs of Avocets, the elegant black and white waders, were found to be nesting here in 1947 after 100 years' absence from Britain. Later that summer, another four pairs were discovered on Havergate Island, near Orford, 12 miles to the south. There was immense interest and excitement as many of our ornithologists had never set eyes on one before. A. W. P. Robertson wrote:

'It was a remarkable occasion, and I cannot remember being more impressed on first acquaintance with a bird. Indeed the media of words and pictures are most inadequate to convey the haunting beauty of the living Avocet. It is black and white, of course, with long slate-blue legs, and a black upturned bill.' And he continued: 'As the avocet walks, each foot is lifted almost to the horizontal before it is advanced and set down again with feline grace and the balance and poise of the bird's movements are a ballerina's despair, exquisite in their perfection.'

The RSPB moved fast: in 1948 Havergate Island was purchased and the local landowner at Minsmere, Captain Stuart Ogilvie, agreed to lease 1500 acres to the Society as a reserve. The Avocet was also chosen as the Society's emblem. At Havergate the birds established a successful although fluctuating colony, but at Minsmere conditions changed and they did not return to breed again until the creation of the Scrape in 1963 provided the right water levels with the plentiful supply of small crustaceans they require.

Another of the reserve's great successes is that the area of reed-marsh has, since 1955, become one of the last strongholds of a very rare British bird – the Marsh Harrier. There are usually $1\frac{1}{2}$ or $2\frac{1}{2}$ nesting pairs at Minsmere – a male is generally bigamous – and in some years these have been the only ones breeding in the country. The female does nearly all the incubating: this lasts up to thirty-eight days and so the male has to supply most of her food. There is often a thrilling display of aerobatics as he approaches the nest with prey and the female takes off to meet him, flipping over on her back to catch the small rodent, bird or Frog he releases from his talons. That other rare marsh bird, the Bittern, also breeds here. There are usually a dozen pairs but this formidable, skulking Heron-like bird requires almost the same nesting conditions as the Marsh Harrier and fierce territorial squabbles frequently occur, to the delight, at least, of the birdwatcher.

One of the smaller star birds of the reed-bed is the Bearded Reedling, or, as it is usually called, the Bearded Tit. In fact it does not belong to the tit family, but is a unique species in Europe. The 'Beardie' is more likely to be heard before it is seen: a metallic 'ching' repeated several times, then a reed-top will sway and there is a sight of an elegant tawny little bird with a long tail and, if it is a male, a blue-grey head and black moustachial stripes.

Grey Herons have also been attracted to the reed-beds and, unusually for Britain, nest here just above water level instead of in high trees. The long list of marshland breeding birds includes Great Crested and Little Grebes, Water Rails and six species of surface-feeding ducks with Gadwall outnumbering Mallard. There are also large numbers of Reed and Sedge Warblers, one or two pairs of Kingfishers, several Cuckoos and Grasshopper Warblers and a few of the newly-colonizing Savi's Warblers.

Owing to concentration of the rare birds on the reed-beds and the Scrape, it is sometimes forgotten that two-thirds of the reserve consist of woodland and heath. Scattered over the low hills that run down to the marsh and around Scott's Hall Farm are some delightful mixtures of oaks, chestnuts, beeches, sycamores and conifers with alders on the wetter ground. The woods were mostly planted in the last century as cover for game-birds. With little or no felling, the natural cycle of growth, death, decay and regeneration has produced excellent feeding and nesting conditions for a large variety of birds. All three British woodpeckers nest, as do Nuthatches and Tree-creepers. There are warblers in abundance, Spotted Flycatchers, all the British tits, except the Crested, and several pairs of Tawny and one or two of Long-eared Owls.

In spring, Nightingales are heard as much by day as by night. In the woods, there are drifts of bluebells and later in the year the undisturbed leaf humus and fallen branches provide ideal conditions for many kinds of fungi. Paths bordering the woods also pass through lanes and scrub, where doves, thrushes, Jays, Greenfinches, Goldfinches, Linnets, Lesser Redpolls, Chaffinches and Yellowhammers are commonly seen. Unfortunately, since 1970, Grey Squirrels have infiltrated and usurped the indigenous Red.

The heathland birds are best seen from the public paths and from the road between the neighbouring villages of Westleton and Dunwich. They include Kestrels, Red-legged and Common Partridges, Meadow and Tree Pipits and an occasional Stonechat. About twenty pairs of Nightjars breed and their churring song can often be heard at dusk in late spring and summer. A thrilling sound that echoes over the heath in early winter is the roar of Red Deer in rut.

Each winter, millions of birds come to Britain's milder climate from the far north and northeast. The varied habitats at Minsmere are attractive to many of these species, and among the regular visitors are Bewick's Swans, Rough-legged Buzzards, Hen Harriers, Great Grey Shrikes and small flocks of Shore Larks, Twites, Snow Buntings and Siskins. Large-scale movements of ducks, geese and gulls can be seen offshore.

The coastal strip of shingle and dunes protects the reserve's low-lying land from the ever-encroaching North Sea, but few birds are able to breed there now owing to disturbance. Some of the worst sufferers are the Little Terns, those 'swallows of the sea'. What a delight it is to watch their elegant, buoyant flight over the waves as they scan the surface, bills downturned. Every now and again one of them will hover daintily on streamlined wings before plummetting down with a splash – to reappear instantly, a tiny fish glinting silver in its yellow bill. In spring, as part of the courtship display, the male will fly around bearing the fish importantly before presenting it to his chosen mate. The nest is a mere scrape in the sand and shingle, and the eggs blend so perfectly that they are almost impossible to see. A holidaymaker walking on the beach might even tread on them without knowing it. Owing to increased pressure on all the beaches round the coast it is sad to think that the graceful Little Tern has now become one of our rarer seabirds. At least, it is good to know that at Minsmere they have found protection and the right breeding conditions created for them. The best news of all is that, as the result of a public appeal in 1977, the RSPB has been able to buy the reserve outright to provide a permanent sanctuary for so many of our threatened birds.

The excellence of the imaginative pioneering work in reserve management carried out at Minsmere has now become an example for all wetland reserves not only in the British Isles but also in Europe. The final accolade came in autumn 1980 when the reserve was awarded the European Diploma of the Council of Europe. This is the first time the award has been won by a nature reserve in Britain run by a voluntary body. Minsmere is indeed a proud feather in the RSPB's cap.

Access By car: off the A12, ½ mile north of Yoxford, via the village of Westleton. By train: to Darsham then by taxi.
Opening times From the beginning of April to 15 September on Sundays, Mondays, Wednesdays and Saturdays 10.30 a.m. to 5 p.m., thereafter to the end of October on Sundays only 10.30 a.m. to 5 p.m. During the rest of the year on Sundays and Wednesdays 10 a.m. to 4.30 p.m.
Permits Available from the reception centre on arrival. The number of permits is limited and they are issued on a first-come, first-served basis.
Facilities Suitable for all the family. There are eight large hides on two main footpaths (each of 2 miles); some of the hides are accessible to the disabled and to cars. A large car park, picnic area, shop, interpretive centre and toilets are provided. On the shore overlooking the reserve are a number of large public hides; these can be reached from Dunwich Cliffs car park.
Warden Minsmere Reserve, Westleton, Saxmundham IP17 2BY. Tel: Westleton 285.

Dunwich Heath

Adjoins Minsmere reserve on north side and is an extension of its heathland and woodland habitats: It is largely owned by the National Trust who maintain a car park on Minsmere Cliff from which excellent sea-watching is possible and from which the RSPB's public hides may be reached by walking ¾ mile along the dunes to the south. Near the car park are a tea shop and toilets.

Walberswick National Nature Reserve

This a large reed-marsh, woodland and sea-shore area managed as a reserve by the Nature Conservancy Council. A network of public footpaths passes through the marsh (Bearded Tit and Marsh Harrier) and other habitats (Nightingale, Nightjar). Shallow pools near the shingle beach are good for waders throughout the year. Terns fish in the River Blyth and there are ducks, waders and herons in the estuary.

Benacre Pits

These are reached via a 2-mile walk north along the shore from the end of the road to Covehithe Church. Here coastal pools are good sites for wintering sea ducks and grebes. There is also good scrub cover for spring and autumn migrants.

Lowestoft Harbour and Ness

England's most easterly point. From March to August there is a Kittiwake colony on the pier and nearby houses and, in autumn and winter, the harbour and offshore are especially good for seabirds and grebes.

Sizewell Beach

Here seabirds feed at the hot-water outlet of the nuclear power station. The area is good for swimming, angling and observing coastal migrants. Black Redstarts breed at this site.

North Warren Reserve RSPB and Thorpeness Mere

At these two areas one can see woodland birds, feeding terns and waterfowl, Nightingales and Cetti's Warbler. Access at all times along marked trail only at North Warren.

Snape Maltings to Iken Church

This stretch of coast comprises wide tidal mudflats where feeding Shelducks and waders, including Avocets, can be seen. The area near Tunstall and Rendlesham Forests is good for woodland birds, including Redstarts and sometimes Crossbills and Woodlarks. The world-famous music centre of the Aldeburgh Festival is at Snape Maltings at the head of the Alde estuary.

CHAPTER TWENTY-ONE

Havergate Island
Nature Reserve, Suffolk
RSPB

Havergate is a flat, desolate strip of shingle and marsh, extending over 270 acres, and is situated at the point where the River Alde suddenly becomes the Ore and forks in two. Suffolk rivers and streams often merge and change their names for no apparent reason; in this case there is some justification as the Ore was once a separate river. The island lies downstream from the gracious old town of Orford, and when first approaching, after the short boat trip from Orford Quay, there is little to be seen: Havergate hides behind embankment walls, which some say were first built up in the 15th century to protect it from flooding. At that time the island consisted of two strips of land used as cattle meadows; they were joined by a shingle bank. Sheep were kept on the island and cattle were swum across for the grazing in summer. Finally, after a pattern of centuries, the enveloping remoteness of the place was shattered by the last war.

In 1940, with invasion expected at any time along this exposed east coast, live shells were fired at the shingle bank in the course of a defence exercise. One of these hit the sluice controlling the smaller of the embanked areas at the southwestern end known as Doveys. The breach widened with every tide and, as the seawater poured in, Doveys, before long, became just a saucer of salty meres and tidal mudflats. As at Minsmere, 12 miles up the coast, the right conditions eventually developed for the return of the Avocet – and all by accident.

In the first years of peace, the dreamy Suffolk shore and coastal marshes were little frequented and it was not until July of the hot, dry summer of 1947 that a local birdwatcher spotted the elegant, unmistakable outlines of the black and white waders flying over Havergate. Four pairs were found to be already breeding on the mudflats in the newly formed lagoons behind the encircling banks. The RSPB was promptly alerted, a group of watchers formed, near wartime security kept, and, as a result, at least eight young successfully fledged.

Meantime, at Minsmere, eight young Avocets also flew from a small colony which had established itself there; they too were closely protected by another group of local people. In fact, so effective was the security, that neither party even told the other.

By the next spring, at both sites, excitement ran high: watchers stood by hoping eagerly for the birds' return. By mid-April, four pairs had returned to Minsmere, but none to Havergate. Nevertheless, over the next fortnight, it became clear that conditions at Minsmere were no longer to the birds' liking: they deserted the site and on 29 April what was presumably the same group turned up on Havergate. A few more birds arrived there and eventually five pairs nested on the island.

It was then that the small band of ornithologists had to face up to the innumerable problems involved in ensuring the little colony's success. First, Rats ate some of the eggs, then Black-headed Gulls took some of the chicks, and, finally in poor weather, only three young fledged. There was better news from the nearby Lantern Marshes where a few pairs succeeded in raising ten young.

Despite the discouragement of this second year, the RSPB decided to take a gamble and purchase Havergate in order to ensure the island's future as a reserve. Management methods were developed there and measures taken to control the predators in the hope of ensuring safe breeding over a larger part of the island.

Then, in 1953, disaster struck. The protecting embankments were breached by a huge tidal surge from the North Sea, driven by the northwesterly gale, which caused the catastrophic east coast floods. Strenuous repair work was carried out as soon as possible to the sea walls, efficient dams and sluices were installed and muddy 'scrapes' with islands constructed on the pattern already successfully pioneered at Minsmere. All this work paid off and over the years a regular colony of some eighty pairs of Avocets became established on Havergate: no wonder the RSPB chose the bird for its emblem and that the island itself is sometimes called, affectionately, Avocet Island.

In spite of their elegant and somewhat delicate appearance, Avocets are in fact hardy birds and sometimes return to their nesting sites as early as February, if there should be a mild spell. Some birds occasionally even spend the winter at Havergate, but their main winter quarters are in the Iberian Peninsula and North Africa, although others overwinter in Devon on the estuary of the Tamar and there are usually about twelve on Brownsea Island in Dorset.

They are without doubt the most distinctive of all waders by reason of their long legs, delicately poised heads and upswept bills. Their plumage is also unmistakable: of purest white with sharply contrasting areas of ebony black on the head, the sides of the back and on the wings. Once heard, the call is never forgotten as when, in graceful flight, with long legs trailing, they utter that wild, musical sound ringing out over the mudflats – 'klu-uit'.

The mating ritual is characteristically charming. First, a pair will draw closer together in a pool where they have been feeding; they preen vigorously and the female then sinks into a soliciting attitude with her chin resting in the water. After a lot of movement behind her, the male mounts, wings held almost vertically to maintain a balance. After mating he slides off forwards; with a gentle deliberation they cross bills, and then walk side by side a few paces, before separating daintily on diagonal paths. Sometimes the male will momentarily stretch one wing across her back, it might seem as though in affection.

Four brown-spotted eggs are laid, usually on the merest scrape in the earth or among thin vegetation, although on occasions the nest can be quite a bulky structure. Both birds take turns incubating and the eggs hatch after twenty-four to twenty-eight days. Within a few hours, the tiny bundles of greyish-brown down are darting about busily. The protective parents lead them off to an area of soft mud where they find their own food of small insects or crustaceans. Within a week, the tiny ½-inch-long bills develop a retroussé tip and they are able to feed like the adults in the most assured manner, swishing their bills from side to side through the shallows and finding their food by touch.

This is their time of greatest danger and the parents then have a frenzied time in defence of their young. Enemies abound and the chicks might so easily be snatched by a Kestrel or gull. It is thanks to the control methods which have been developed that the colony of Black-headed Gulls on the island, once 4000 strong, has been much reduced. Nevertheless, predators still take a toll of Avocet chicks and also of the young of Common and Sandwich Terns.

Among the breeding colony of Common Terns, one or two pairs of Arctic Terns nest, but it is a challenge to pick them out in the throng. The Arctics are a little greyer and have shorter legs than their near relation; another distinction is that the bill is all red, while the Common Tern has a red bill with a black tip. At Havergate the Arctic is on the southern limit of its breeding range in Britain and only one or two other pairs are known to nest, irregularly, elsewhere in the southern half of England.

Out on the little islands and mud of the lagoons there is a wide variety of birds to be seen feeding or nesting. Conspicuous among them are a few Canada Geese and several pairs of Shelducks. Gulls seem to be everywhere: in addition to the colony of Black-headed, many larger, non-breeding gulls stand around loafing or preening. They are mostly Herring and Lesser Black-backed Gulls; 3000 pairs nest near the lighthouse on Orford Ness across the river.

In the breeding season all is hustle and bustle as nervous Avocets, Oystercatchers, Redshanks and Ringed Plovers attack everything that comes near their nests or chicks. Black-headed Gulls with loud cries chase the smaller and more elegant terns, hoping to make them drop the tiny fish they are bringing in to their mates or young; these bullies are, in turn, chased by the larger gulls, which are also ever-ready to snatch up a straying chick.

Meantime, in the deep wide ditches below the embankment into which the hides are built, dapper black and white Tufted Ducks dive quietly for their food, seemingly unaffected by the turmoil. Neither is the Short-eared Owl, which glides and hunts in slow, flapping flight, searching for voles and keeping well out of it.

By mid-summer, relative calm returns to the lagoons. Migrant ducks and waders arrive from the north and are soon busy feeding. There are fussy little flocks of Dunlin, courtly Black-tailed and Bar-tailed Godwits and smaller numbers of Green, Wood, Curlew and Common Sandpipers. The male Ruffs are now bereft of their splendid breeding plumage and move about quietly with the smaller reeves. New wild cries are now heard over the marsh: the distinctive calls of Grey Plovers, Curlews, Whimbrels, Greenshanks and Spotted Redshanks. Most of these birds move on, but, as autumn merges into winter, Mallard, Gadwall, Teal and Shoveler, a few of which will have bred, also Wigeon and Pintail, steadily build up their numbers. In hard weather, White-fronted Geese and family parties of Bewick's and Whooper Swans can be expected. Throughout the winter there are waterfowl, gulls and some waders; all the year round, Havergate remains an island of birds.

Apart from birds, there is little to see. A few traces remain of earlier days: close to the path between the hides are the rusting remains of machinery – once used in an attempt to set up a shingle extraction industry. Here, too, are the remains of a brick cottage. The one-time inhabitants, up to the 1920s, tended cattle and cultivated corn and vegetables: they left behind a fine specimen remaining today of the Duke of Argyll's tea-plant.

Gorse and mallow add colour to the shingle and grassy ridges near the warden's huts; sea aster flourishes in the saltings near the high-water mark, where the delicate tendrils and purple flowers of the rare sea pea appear miraculously among the pebbles.

From the hides, the view across the muddy lagoons is backed by distant woods on the higher ground above Gedgrave marshes on the mainland. Soaring above all and forever catching the eye is the great 90-foot tower of Henry II's Orford Castle. This was completed in

1173 to help Henry control the East Anglian barons. For 200 years it served as a key fortress and remained intact until the 1600s. Now, only the great twelve-sided keep remains on its green hillock, but it is well worth a visit as there is none other like it in Britain. There are three rectangular turrets; two of them contain rooms all the way up, including kitchens. The third has a spiral staircase and the climb is rewarded at the top by commanding views over the rolling Suffolk countryside.

Access From the A12 at Woodbridge by-pass, minor roads lead eastward to Orford. They pass through remnants of the great forest of oaks and hollies that covered this part of Suffolk in medieval times. The most direct road is not perhaps the most scenic, although there may be Crossbills on the fringes of the large dark blocks of Forestry Commission pines. Meet on Orford Quay at time shown on instruction sheet. Boat trip takes about ½ hour. Suitable for all the family. Warm clothing advisable.

Opening times From the beginning of April to the end of August on Saturdays, Sundays and Mondays all day (9 a.m. to 5 p.m.) and on Thursdays half-day visits, morning or afternoon. Limited visiting from November to February – dates from the warden.

Permits By written application. Charges: £1 members, £2 non-members.

Warden 30 Mundays Lane, Orford, Woodbridge, Suffolk IP12 2LX.

CHAPTER TWENTY-TWO

Northward Hill
National Nature Reserve, Kent
RSPB

The reserve consists of 135 acres of dense scrub and mixed woodland close to the village of High Halstow near Rochester. From the heights it looks out over the North Kent marshes on the south side of the Thames estuary – just 38 miles along the A2 from London. Small it may be, yet it holds the largest heronry in Britain with around 220 pairs, although the number fluctuates from year to year. When ponds, ditches and wetlands freeze over, the Herons are cut off from their food supply and then they disperse, in the hope of finding milder conditions. The total population for Britain usually varies between 5000 and 7000 pairs although, following the long freeze of 1963, they were reduced to 2000 pairs and recovery was slow.

It was in 1900 that the first of the great grey birds nested at Northward Hill and a colony soon built up. Since then a small housing estate has also built up alongside the reserve. As Herons are sensitive birds when nesting and, if disturbed, readily fly off leaving the eggs and chicks exposed to predators, it has been necessary to divide the reserve into two parts: a sanctuary area to which there is no public access; and a large area of tangled scrub with a network of paths, which is open at all times.

From a high viewing point set in a tree among the scrub up on the hill it is possible to look down the wooded slope to the left, where the heronry is set among oaks and hawthorns. In this way, a small part of the sanctuary area can be viewed in March or early April before the leaves are on the trees. Unless the weather is exceptionally severe, the Herons begin to arrive back at their old nests by late January. These are large structures, often perched precariously at the tops of the tallest trees, and the ungainly birds carry out the necessary repairs with surprising agility. The male does most of the stick collecting and on his return there is a dignified little ceremony involving neck stretching and mutual billing and caressing until, crest-raised, he proffers his gift to the female, who then builds it into the nest. Clutches of three to five greenish-blue eggs are laid usually in March, incubation lasts twenty-five days, and most of the young are able to fly by mid-May, although some may still be present a month later.

At Northward Hill, the birds are most often seen when flying to and from the colony. In flight, the long neck is drawn right back and the legs trail behind. The wingbeats are slow and may appear ponderous, yet a Heron can travel at thirty miles per hour and is surprisingly agile.

Down on the marshes adjoining the reserve, there is a chance of watching one of these most patient of fishermen exercising his skills. He is a versatile feeder and in addition to fish and eels will take crabs, prawns, frogs, mice, small birds, grasshoppers, waterbeetles, and, in severe weather, might add the occasional rat to his bill of fare. On the ground, he is seen to be a rather sober-looking bird: his plumage of grey and white streaked with black and the long dark crest giving him a look of refined distinction. The yellow, pick-axe bill has slight serrations on both mandibles, so that, once grabbed, the prey is in a vice. The stilt-like legs are ideal for wading and his unwebbed feet are huge with long spidery toes to prevent him from sinking in soft mud. The female has duller colouring and a shorter crest: less striking, at least in appearance.

It is quite a spectacle to watch a Heron swallowing an Eel. Once grabbed, the Eel thrashes about, often entwining itself around the bird's neck in a determined attempt to avoid the inevitable. This delaying action may last several minutes before the Heron can manage to get the Eel head-first into its bill and swallow it alive. The still wriggling Eel then becomes no more than a bulge, moving slowly down the inside of the long neck.

In the struggle, the Heron usually gets a great deal of slime on its feathers. Cleaning up afterwards is a lengthy business. First, the bird extracts a powdery substance with the tip of its bill from glands positioned above the tail. It then spreads this methodically over the sticky places. The resultant mess is slowly removed by what is in effect a built-in comb – the deeply-serrated edge of the long claw of the third toe.

Apart from affording a glimpse of the heronry, the public scrub areas themselves are rewarding to visit, especially in April or May. Northward Hill then becomes a wonderful place for birdsong. Close to the heronry, there is a large colony of raucous Rooks, but, in contrast, further up the hill, are heard the Nightingales' marvellous throbbing notes. They sing, of course, by day as well as by night and there are usually around twenty pairs. The males arrive from their winter quarters in tropical Africa about mid-April and the females follow 10 days later. The cock is the singer. With patience, there is a fair chance of seeing the little red-brown bird. At close quarters, its underneath is greyish-white with pale buff colour on the breast; the tail is russet – similar to a Redstart's. Like the Redstart too the Nightingale is something of a ventriloquist; the voice seems to come from everywhere at once. By this means, the cocks may well be able to control larger territories.

In May many other birds sing among the tangled greenery with its drifts of bluebells and red campion. There is a good variety of the common warblers and also hole-nesting birds including Great Spotted Woodpeckers, Great and Blue Tits. The drowsy crooning of Turtle Doves provides the perfect background for the songsters; there are several pairs of our smallest breeding doves on the reserve. It is a slim bird with reddish-brown upperparts mottled with black; the breast is pink, there is a black and white striped patch on the neck and the tail is long with a white tip. Close to, the Turtle Dove's eye is seen to be rimmed with dull red.

One pair of Long-eared Owls is known to breed at Northward

Hill and a few others roost there by day outside the breeding season. There is a far better chance of seeing a Little Owl, as this flies by day with a noticeably bounding flight and occasional hovering. The species was introduced from the continent in the last century and rapidly became established; there are about 10 pairs on the reserve.

In winter, birds here are scarcer, although there is a good chance of seeing geese – White-fronts and Brent. The best vantage point is the treetop hide overlooking the marshes. From here, it may also be possible to see Hen Harriers, Merlins and Short-eared Owls. At any time of year, it is well worth while combining a visit to the reserve with a walk down by the river: the Thames-side salty mud-flats provide excellent feeding for thousands of ducks and waders.

A visit is also advised to the ancient cathedral city of Rochester, a few miles away, on the lower reaches of the River Medway. The city has many associations with Charles Dickens and features in his novels, especially *Pickwick Papers* and *Great Expectations*. The area is steeped in history: there was a settlement here even before Roman times. The Norman castle has a 125 foot-high keep; the walls in places being thirteen feet thick.

Access From London leave the A2 at Strood. This is at the junction with the M2. Turn left on to A289, then take the A228 signed to Grain. After four miles turn left on to minor road, Christmas Lane, and continue for another mile to the village of High Halstow. A path leads to the reserve from Northwood Avenue. Car park at Village Hall. (It is planned to build a Reserve Display Centre with a car park at some time in the future.)
Opening times The public area is open at all times. No charge and no permit required. Owing to the proximity of a housing estate and pressure of visitors in summer, week-ends are best avoided if possible. A week-day visit early in the morning is ideal.
Facilities Suitable for all the family, although it must be stressed that this is a fine weather reserve. When wet, the network of paths is well-nigh impassable, owing to the slithery clay mud. Even with rubber boots, the going is then very difficult.
Warden Swigshole Cottage, High Halstow, Rochester, Kent ME3 8SR.

CHAPTER TWENTY-THREE

Stodmarsh National Nature Reserve, Kent

Nature Conservancy Council

It is not often that man's interference with the crust of his earth results in an improvement of wildlife habitat. The National Coal Board has been blamed for many ugly scars and dumps, but at Stodmarsh, albeit unwittingly, it has produced a splendid little marshland of shallow meres, partially flooded grassland and reed-beds – the type of habitat so rich in birds and, because of widespread drainage, so scarce.

The National Nature Reserve's 406 wetland acres were slowly formed on the south flank of the Great Stour River, five miles north-east of Canterbury, as meadowland, criss-crossed with ditches, subsided over underground coal workings. The shallow meres thus created had a rich floor of drowned grass and topsoil which had long been fertilized by grazing cattle. Reeds and rushes spread rapidly from the ditches; sallows, alders and hawthorns flourished on the banks and a variety of birds readily colonized the new habitat.

To protect this important area and ensure its future management, the Nature Conservancy Council established a reserve there in 1968, acquiring the freehold of the eastern half and arranging a management agreement over the remainder with the owners, Coal

Industries Estates Ltd. The reserve is centrally divided by the Lampen Wall, an old flood-defence embankment which makes an excellent elevated public path through the reed-beds and meres and proceeds along the south side of the pretty river.

Stodmarsh is the nearest fresh-water marsh to the Continent and, as might be expected, was the first British site to be re-colonized by Savi's Warbler when it began to increase its numbers in France soon after the end of the Second World War. This little summer resident, named after the Italian ornithologist who first described the species in 1824, is dependent upon wet beds of reeds and rushes and had bred commonly in East Anglia's extensive fenland until the middle of the last century, when it disappeared. In this south east corner of England, Savi's Warbler is on the edge of its European breeding range, and its failure to return each spring to nest here was probably due to a natural periodic contraction of its distribution, accelerated by loss of much of its specialized habitat through drainage.

A hundred years after its disappearance, a few Savi's Warblers were seen at Stodmarsh; and a decade or so later scattered pairs also began breeding in North Kent, Devon and East Anglia. The total British population is still very small and unstable.

Savi's Warbler is a skulking bird, inhabiting tall, densely-grown reed-beds with a scattering of rushes. It is somewhat nondescript in appearance, with plain olive-brown upperparts, a little warmer in tone than the very similarly-plumaged Reed Warbler which also breeds, in larger numbers, at Stodmarsh. Its chief feature is its song – an unbirdlike reel, as if made by a little, fast-running sewing-machine and even that can be confused with the song of another of Stodmarsh's reed-bed residents, the Grasshopper Warbler.

For all but the most expert, it is just as well that the embankment which runs through the reserve offers the best chance in Britain of seeing small and elusive marshland birds. From the tall reeds on one side, they seem to like to fly across the path to hunt for food along a ditch or pond edge on the other side or to use one of the bankside trees as a song perch. The sallows and alders are also unrivalled in offering good opportunities to see Cetti's Warbler, another small marsh bird named after an Italian ornithologist, that is new to Britain in post-war years. Non-migratory and resident once it had arrived here from across the Channel, it was affected by persistent cold in winter and was slow to establish itself. Then, from the early 1970s, the long period of milder winters enabled it to survive, breed successfully and spread to many more marshes in southern England; but nowhere has it yet become so numerous as it is at Stodmarsh.

While still normally a skulking bird, Cetti's Warbler announces its presence with an extraordinarily explosive '*whi*chew, *whi*chew, *whi*chew chew chew chew chew' repeated every few minutes from the middle of a waterside tree or a tangle of reeds and bramble, its favourite haunt. Having got over his surprise at this outburst, the birdwatcher should stand still and give himself the chance of a good view of this bird in the bush before it moves off to declare possession of another part of its wide territory. Superficially like other small song-birds of the marshland, it is more red-brown above and greyer below than a Reed or Savi's Warbler and has a more distinctly rounded tail.

Another Stodmarsh speciality to be seen here, and very different with its buff, black and white plumage and longish tail, is the Bearded Tit. Good numbers nest on this reserve and influxes occur during the period of eruptive movements in late autumn and, more erratically, in winter when hard weather may cause flocks to move from marsh to marsh in search of food. Stodmarsh was one of the main sites in which a new, steady breeding population developed after the birds spread from East Anglia in 1959.

A wide variety of other marshland birds, ranging from Bitterns to Reed Buntings and including Great Crested and Little Grebes, seven common species of ducks and a few Garganey, nest on this lovely little reserve. That they all, with their different nesting and feeding requirements, are able to do so, is due to careful management by the resident warden. Water levels are carefully maintained, beds of reed, sedges and rush kept within bounds by rotational cutting and burning, and the wet meadows are prevented from turning into scrubland by seasonal cattle grazing. Suitable habitats for a wide variety of marshland plants, including interesting species like bladder-wort, bogbean, frogbit and flowering rush, are also thus provided. These controlled, protected conditions invite many birds to spend the winter here. Wigeon, Mallard, Teal and Shoveler are common on the flooded meadows and Tufted Duck and Pochard can be seen, with grebes, diving in the deeper meres. Marsh and Hen Harriers occur on spring and autumn migration and occasionally also in winter. An Osprey, on its way to or from Scotland or Scandinavia, sometimes stays to fish, as do several species of terns. Lapwings, Redshanks and Snipe, which also breed here, are especially numerous in winter when Ruffs and Black-tailed Godwits too may be watched feeding out on the wet meadows or around the edges of the pools.

Perhaps this new marsh represents the wetland wilderness that existed here in the Stour Valley in the days when Canterbury, a few miles upstream, was not the bustling city that it is today. Originally a Saxon settlement on an important river crossing, it became a fortress when Roman invaders, following the Stour inland from their landing in Pegwell Bay, established a permanent encampment here in AD 43. Then, the most important event in the town's long history, it became the cradle from which Christianity spread throughout England after King Ethelbert of Kent was baptized here by St Augustine in AD 597.

Nothing survives of the first cathedral that was then built by the godly emissary from Rome. Now, the Bell Harry tower soars above the world-famous cathedral that was begun on its site in 1067 and lives on to play its vital role in England's history. Henry II walked here barefoot in penance for the murder, in 1170, of Thomas Beckett, his 'turbulent priest' and began the pilgrimages to Canterbury which lasted until Beckett's shrine was destroyed in 1538 during Henry VIII's Dissolution of the Monasteries.

Through this ancient city, the Stour winds its way past Stodmarsh reserve down to its mouth in the Channel where the Continent is only some twenty-five miles away – a short crossing much used by the millions of migrant birds that come to Britain for the winter. Close by, a strategically-sited bird observatory is kept busy at the coast near the old Cinque Port of Sandwich.

Access Leave Canterbury going east on A257 and after a mile turn left on the minor road for another 3½ miles to Stodmarsh. From the Red Lion Inn in the middle of the village, a short country lane leads to the reserve car park, from which the walk across the Lampen Wall begins. The reserve is open at all times and there is no permit fee. Terrain suitable for all the family. Further information from The Warden, 'Reedlings', Stodmarsh, Canterbury, Kent.

CHAPTER TWENTY-FOUR

Dungeness Reserve, Kent
RSPB

There is nowhere in the world like Dungeness. A vast desert of stones, bleak, inhospitable, mysterious, pointing like an arrowhead at France's Cap Gris Nez, 26 miles across the water, and marking the southern end of that most congested of shipping lanes – the Strait of Dover. Four thousand years have gone to make this great headland of flint pebbles covering nearly 8 square miles, and jutting 3 miles further into the sea than when the Romans first invaded Britain; incongruously, looming overall, is one of Britain's largest nuclear power stations.

The shingle has been built up by eastward drift, the action of countless waves which had first torn the pebbles as rocks from the cliffs to the west. It has been a long, complicated process about which there has been much controversy but it is known to have speeded up after the 13th century, when the mouth of the River Rother shifted course from Romney, finally joining the sea to the west of Dungeness at Rye.

The changing position of the coastline can be clearly seen from the low ridges of shingle banked up in succession. For this reason, it has become world-famous to students of coastal formations and of

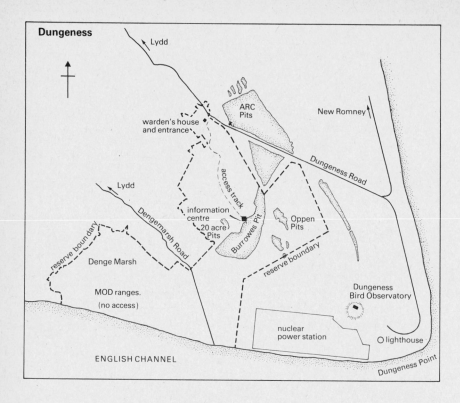

Dungeness

Lydd

ARC Pits

New Romney

warden's house and entrance

Dungeness Road

Lydd

access track

Dengemarsh Road

information centre

20 acre Pits

Burrowes Pit

Oppen Pits

reserve boundary

reserve boundary

Denge Marsh

Dungeness Bird Observatory

MOD ranges.
(no access)

nuclear power station

O lighthouse

ENGLISH CHANNEL

Dungeness Point

great interest also to naturalists, who are able to give an exact date to the particular area of shore they happen to be studying.

But perhaps the most remarkable thing about Dungeness is that it has been able to survive in any way at all as a reserve. During the war, it was taken over by the army as an extension of the firing range at Lydd; some of the best areas are still a mortar range. At the turn of the century, it was nothing but a stony desert, although there was a full-sized railway operating through the middle of the Ness taking away gravel for ballast. There were then vast breeding colonies of Black-headed Gulls and Common Terns.

The rare Stone Curlew and Kentish Plover also bred in small numbers on the shingle. For this reason, the RSPB decided in 1907 to employ a warden here. Dungeness has the distinction of being the Society's oldest reserve, which it purchased in 1929, although the entire 1200 acres did not become its property until 1956.

It was feared the reserve would be ruined when the nuclear power station was constructed near the Point a few years later. There has certainly been great disturbance; Stone Curlews and other birds have lost their breeding sites and the pylons and cables take their toll of birds. Fortunately, another industrial enterprise has been turned to the reserve's advantage. The vast mineral wealth of shingle had rather surprisingly not been exploited until near the end of the last century when gravel-quarrying began. By the 1930s, with mechanization, huge pits were being excavated to depths of 30 feet. These soon became freshwater lakes, often with islands of unwanted sand and silt.

It was in these havens that the gulls and terns sought refuge, when wartime activity, followed by predation from Foxes and Crows, drove them off their nesting sites on the open shingle. In fact, to a large extent, Dungeness has finally been saved as a reserve through co-operation between the gravel companies and the RSPB: the companies get the gravel, the RSPB get the royalties, and the birds get excellent new nesting conditions with full protection.

Let us look more closely at this unique reserve which has survived an industrial revolution. We approach it from the little town of Lydd, once on the coast, now lying 3 miles inland. An explosive was first tested here on the army ranges – Lyddite. There is a fine church, dating back to the 14th century, with a 130-foot tower looking out over Walland Marsh and nearby is a wooded park with a heronry. About $1\frac{1}{2}$ miles along the road to Dungeness is the warden's house, the 400-year-old Boulderwall Farm, and the entrance to the reserve.

In all, forty-five species breed here regularly – not a great number, but then this is a highly specialized area and could not be expected to support a large variety of birds. Nevertheless, in recent years, some 270 species have been recorded. The gravel pits are being excavated to a carefully designed plan so as to leave islands, shallows and gentle slopes for hundreds of nesting, resting and feeding birds. Black-headed Gulls and Common Terns have thriving colonies on the islands; and Great Crested Grebes, Shelduck, Mallard and Tufted Duck nest around the margins of the gravel pit lakes. In winter this is a good place to see Northern Grebes and Sawbills, including Smew and some 3000 other ducks of various species.

Dungeness has the distinction of being the only regular breeding site in England of the Common Gull. In spite of the name, its nesting sites in Britain are normally confined to Scotland and parts of Ireland; but here about twelve pairs are scattered throughout the promontory each year. They look like small Herring Gulls, except that their legs are yellow-green instead of pink and the yellow bill lacks the red spot.

A bird now becoming quite rare as a breeding species in south-east England is the beautifully marked Wheatear. In the 19th century they were prized as table delicacies; around Eastbourne alone the average number trapped was about 22,000 each year. The name probably has nothing to do with grain, but is thought to come, more basically, from the Anglo-Saxon 'White Arse', referring to the male bird's brilliant white rump, contrasting with its french-grey back. The tail pattern is most distinctive; white sides with the centre and terminal area black like an inverted letter T. They most often nest in rabbit burrows, but as there is none among the stones, artificial sites have been provided for them by burying pipes and boxes in the ground. The Wheatears have accepted these gratefully and good numbers of them are now able to breed.

Near the Point, there are some unique natural features of the reserve. The vast accumulation of stones 13 feet deep on a bed of clay is a great catchment area of rain water. At Dungeness this is never far below the surface, so that some remarkable inland hollows, formed by arms of shingle raised by storms in ancient times, have now become ponds, overgrown with reeds and sallow. The largest of these, the Twenty Acre and the Oppen (meaning open water) Pits are the only areas of natural freshwater on Dungeness and possibly the only freshwater on a shingle formation anywhere in the world. Thanks to their isolated situation, they are of particular interest to naturalists.

One oddity is the Marsh Frog, Europe's largest amphibian, 5 inches long, greenish-brown and very noisy. A small number was brought from Hungary and released on Romney Marsh in 1935 and, while they have multiplied exceedingly here, they have not spread to other parts of Britain. Their food consists of insects, worms and small fish. They will also take the young of small mammals and birds and have unfortunately nearly eliminated the smaller Common Frog.

The wildest area of the reserve is now the western part and there are good views from the little dead-end roads that run from Lydd to the shore at Dengemarsh. No wonder that there is a saying: the world consists of five continents and Romney Marsh.

Among the birds nesting in the sparse vegetation of the shingle are Red-legged and Common Partridges, Pied and Yellow Wagtails, Skylarks, Meadow Pipits, Corn Buntings and Linnets. Birds which breed on the bare stones, especially Herring Gulls and the elegant Little Terns, suffer greatly from predation by Foxes and Carrion Crows. Owing to the lack of trees, the Crows have taken to nesting high up on pylons leading from the nuclear power station or sometimes in low bushes. One year the warden found a Crow's nest with large young in a hawthorn only 6 feet high. Underneath, to one side, a House Sparrow had a nest with eggs and on the other side, only a few inches away, a Tree Sparrow had a nest with young. Magpies are also numerous, and sometimes have to nest only 1½ feet from the ground. Long-eared Owls use some of the old nests.

Dungeness is also an exceptional place for insects. Some beetles and bugs are scarcely found anywhere else, while its breeding moths include the Toadflax Brocade, Notched Emerald, Tawny Shears and a unique yellow form of the Grass Eggar. In addition, there are five species of hawk moth and others, including Hummingbird and Death's Head Moths, can be seen as migrants. The Essex Skipper is the rarest of the few butterflies which breed here, but there are clouds of migrants, especially Red Admirals, Peacocks, Painted Ladies and Whites.

Broom and blackthorn have adapted to the tearing winds by growing in low clumps, and there are long, groundhugging tendrils of bramble. The temperature on the stones is high and so the fruits ripen early: in summer it is strange to see on the shingle cover-loving birds like Whitethroats, Garden Warblers and Nightingales feeding on the berries. Other warblers, Goldcrests, Firecrests and flycatchers hunt busily for insects and spiders in isolated clumps of straggly gorse.

The brown and grey stony wastes show some colour in spring

and early summer with blue drifts of viper's bugloss mingling with the white of Nottingham catchfly, the pink and mauve of foxglove and thrift. They are in striking contrast to the olive-drabness of wood sage and mats of crunchy lichen, clinging to the low ridges where the shingle is finer.

Approaching the Point, we find a mass of creamy white sea kale, the elegant yellow horned poppy, curled dock, sorrel and orache – the first plants to take hold in this salt-sprayed land of stones. In autumn and winter, flocks of larks, finches and buntings feed on the seeds; and many other birds shelter here against the fierce winds which tear across at any time of the year.

Dungeness is one of the best places in Britain from which to study migration. This is because of the short sea crossing, the southern location, the right-angle bend in the coastline and the grounding of night migrants in bad weather. Early this century, ornithologists such as H. G. Alexander and N. F. Ticehurst started recording the big movements and rarities to be seen here. Then in 1952 a group of enthusiasts from Kent, Sussex and London set up a bird observatory, with its headquarters in a block of coastguard cottages sheltering behind an embankment of shingle near the old lighthouse, ½ mile from the Point. The Observatory works closely with the British Trust for Ornithology and is one of a chain in Britain and western Europe where visitors may stay and assist in the work of trapping, ringing and recording the movements of land and sea birds. After a starless night, when small migrants have been unable to navigate, the scattered bushes at the Point can be alive with Willow Warblers, Whitethroats, Redstarts, chats and flycatchers. As many as 687 small birds have been caught and ringed in one day here and more than 10,000 in a year. In all, more than 290 species have been seen including several 'firsts' for Britain.

The Ness juts out into water 10 fathoms deep, so there's a grandstand view of ships of all sizes passing close offshore. At low-tide, the long, shallow bays on either side become mile-wide stretches of sand, where gulls and terns rest and flocks of Curlews, godwits, sandpipers and other waders feed. There is a vigorous tide and the well-scoured waters at the Point and westward are much favoured by anglers; also by grebes, divers, auks and sea ducks from

Arctic breeding grounds. Dungeness is a splendid place for sea-watching and there is a good hide ashore at the observatory. The offshore uprush of hot water from the power station's cooling system ensures a plentiful supply of seafood, brought to the surface by the turbulence. This so-called 'Patch' attracts a wide variety of seabirds, including many Little Gulls and Black Terns, the piratical skuas and occasionally some rarities such as the Mediterranean Gull and the White-winged Black Tern. Here, an offshoot of advanced nuclear technology is, indirectly, of benefit to birds.

In autumn there are few better places than Dungeness Point from which to watch the arrival of huge flocks of Blackbirds, Fieldfares, Redwings, Skylarks and Starlings from the Continent. Meantime, smaller parties of pipits, wagtails and finches which will have followed the coastline down from the north, can be seen departing on their long, adventurous journeys to winter quarters in southwest France, Portugal and Spain.

Access Off the Lydd to Dungeness road; the reserve is $1\frac{1}{2}$ miles from Lydd, the observatory 4 miles. Car parking space at each site.
Opening times The RSPB reserve is open every Wednesday, Thursday, Saturday and Sunday from 10.30 a.m. to 5 p.m. – report to the information centre first. It is likely to be closed mid-week in winter – check with the warden. The observatory is open all year, all day, every day.
Facilities Suitable for all the family. On the reserve there is a visitors' trail with hides.
Accommodation Rather spartan dormitory accommodation with self-catering is available by prior arrangement at the observatory – apply to the observatory warden.
Warden RSPB Reserve, Boulderwall Farm, Dungeness Road, Lydd, Kent, TN29 9PN/Dungeness Bird Observatory, Coastguard Cottages, Dungeness, Romney Marsh, Kent.

Other sites:

The whole of Romney Marsh and adjacent flatlands from Pett Level near Fairlight Cliffs and Hastings in the southwest, to Hythe in the north and Appledore in the northwest is good birding country

throughout the year. It is also full of history. Here is the centre of the
12th-century Cinque Ports – the 'Antiente Townes' of Rye and
Winchelsea added as the sixth and seventh – which made and
supplied ships for the first British Navy, when most of what is now
Romney Marsh was under the sea. Later, defence against the French
was provided by Henry VIII's Camber Castle, built in 1538 and now
inhabited by Kestrels, Stock Doves and Jackdaws. The Martello
Towers on either side of Dymchurch-under-the-Wall were built to
counter the threat of Napoleon and have been a haunt of real-life
smugglers, as well as of Dr Syn and his cronies. Inland, Romney
Marsh is bordered by the Royal Military Canal, which with its
accompanying long line of trees and water plants is easily followed
along a quiet road, providing good birdwatching from Hythe to
Iden Lock, near Rye.

Rye itself is well worth a visit. The town stands on high ground
overlooking the flat lands from which the sea has receded. The
harbour is now at the mouth of the Rother nearly 2 miles away.
There are many Elizabethan houses some of which have Georgian
fronts. The 15th-century Mermaid Inn was once used as a
headquarters by smugglers who are said to have sat at tables with
loaded pistols in open defiance of the Customs men.

The American author Henry James lived in nearby Lamb House,
an 18th-century mansion, from 1898 until his death in 1916. There is
also a 12th-century church with a 16th-century turret clock thought
to be the oldest in the country.

Rye Harbour Local Nature Reserve East Sussex County Council/Sussex Trust for Nature Conservation

This is another, smaller (250 acres) shingle and gravel-pit reserve,
interestingly situated against the west side of the mouth of the River
Rother. Here the last regularly nesting pair of Kentish Plovers in
Britain bred in 1956. Conservation work is continuing in the hope
that the species will return to breed here. The river and broad sands
attract many birds and from a public hide there are views of a lake
and islands, where Common Terns and Black-headed Gulls nest and

where many waders, ducks and other water birds roost during migration and in winter. Among some fifty species breeding on the reserve are also Ringed Plovers, Oystercatchers, Redshanks, Little Terns and Yellow Wagtails. Further information (and annual report) from The Warden, 1 Coastguard Cottages, Rye Harbour, Rye, Sussex.

Pett Level Pools

Situated about 2 miles west of Rye Harbour, these provide excellent birdwatching sites beside the coastal road between Winchelsea Beach and Cliff End. Water levels are controlled to provide good feeding conditions for waders, ducks, swans and grebes. The sandy shore and sheep meadows are also much used by birds.

CONSERVATION ORGANIZATIONS
IN THE BRITISH ISLES

In addition to our personal selection of bird reserves included in this book there are hundreds of others, some large, some small, throughout the country. They and other wildlife areas are in the care of a wide range of organizations who are always glad of enquiries and new members. Those mainly concerned with birdlife are:

Army Bird Watching Society, Candlewick Cottage, Avenue Road, Fleet, Hants GU13 8NG

Association for the Protection of Rural Scotland, 20 Falkland Avenue, Newton Nairn, Renfrewshire G77 5DR

British Association for Shooting and Conservation, Marford Mill, Rossett, Clwyd LL13 0AW

British Naturalists' Association, c/o The Society for the Protection of Ancient Buildings, 55 Great Ormond Street, London WC1

British Ornithologists' Union, c/o The Zoological Society of London, Regent's Park, London NW1 4RY

British Trust for Conservation Volunteers, 10–14 Duke Street, Reading, Berks RG1 4RU

British Trust for Ornithology, Beech Grove, Tring, Herts HP23 5NR

Channel Islands Bird Ringing Scheme, Societe Jersiaise, 9 Pier Road, St Helier, Jersey

Countryside Commission, John Dower House, Crescent Place, Cheltenham, Glos GL50 3RA

Countryside Commission for Scotland, Battleby, Redgorton, Perth PH1 3EW

Countryside Commission, Committee for Wales, 8 Broad Street, Newton, Powys, Wales. SY16 2LU

Department of the Environment for Northern Ireland, Stormont, Belfast BT4 3SS

Edward Grey Institute of Field Ornithology, Department of Zoology, South Parks Road, Oxford OX1 3PS

Farming and Wildlife Advisory Group, The Lodge, Sandy, Beds SG19 2DL

Fauna and Flora Preservation Society, c/o Zoological Society of London, Regents Park, London NW1 4RY

Field Studies Council, Preston Montford, Montford Bridge, Shrewsbury SY4 1HW (runs nine courses at centres in England and Wales)

Forestry Commission, 231 Corstorphine Road, Edinburgh EH12 7AT

Game Conservancy, Burgate Manor, Fordingbridge, Hants SP6 1EF

Hawk Trust, Loton Park, Shrewsbury, Shropshire

International Council for Bird Preservation, 219c Huntingdon Road, Cambridge CB3 0DL

Irish Wildbird Conservancy, c/o Royal Irish Academy, 19 Dawson Street, Dublin 2

National Trust, 42 Queen Anne's Gate, London SW1H 9AS

Nature Conservancy Council (Headquarters), 20 Belgrave Square, London SW1X 8PY

    Headquarters for England: Calthorpe House, Calthorpe Street, Banbury, Oxon OX16 8EX

    Headquarters for Scotland: 12 Hope Terrace, Edinburgh EH9 2AS.

    Headquarters for Wales: Plas Penrhos, Penrhos Road, Bangor, Gwynedd LL57 2LQ

Northern Ireland Bird Records Committee, 9 Dillons Avenue, Whiteabbey, Newtonabbey, Co. Antrim, N. Ireland

Rare Breeding Birds Panel, Fountains, Park Lane, Blunham, Beds MK44 3NJ

Royal Air Force Ornithological Society, c/o MOD Defence Lands 3, Room 768, Tolworth Tower, Ewell Road, Surbiton, Surrey KT6 7DR

Royal Naval Birdwatching Society, Melrose, 23 St David's Road, Southsea, Hants PO5 1QH

Royal Society for Nature Conservation, The Green, Nettleham, Lincoln LN2 2NR (the national association of the 42 regional [mainly county] Nature Conservation Trusts)

Royal Society for the Prevention of Cruelty to Animals, The Causeway, Horsham, West Sussex RH12 1HG

Royal Society for the Protection of Birds, The Lodge, Sandy, Beds SG19 2DL maintains 90 reserves throughout UK and nine regional offices including:

    Scotland – 17 Regent Terrace, Edinburgh
    N. Ireland – Belvoir Park Forest, Belfast
    Wales – 18 High Street, Newtown, Powys SY16 1AA

Scottish Field Studies Association, Kindrogan Field Centre, Enochdhu, Blairgowrie, Perthshire PH10 7PG

Scottish Ornithologists' Club, 21 Regent Terrace, Edinburgh EH7 5BN

Scottish Wildlife Trust, 25 Johnston Terrace, Edinburgh EH1 2NH

Seabird Group, Zoology Department, The University, Sheffield S10 2TN

Ulster Trust for Nature Conservation, 24 Malone Park, Belfast BT9 6NJ, N. Ireland

Watch, 22 The Green, Nettleham, Lincoln LN2 2NR (Junior section of RSNC, q.v.)

Water Space Amenity Commission, 1 Queen Anne's Gate, London SW1H 9BT (for information about birdwatching at reservoirs)

Wildlife Trust, Slimbridge, Gloucester GL2 7BT (maintains six other wildfowl refuges in England and Scotland). Also headquarters of the International Waterfowl Research Bureau.

World Wildfowl Fund – UK. 29 Greville Street, London EC1N 8AX

Young Ornithologists' Club, RSPB, The Lodge, Sandy, Beds SG19 2DL

Zoological Society of London, Regent's Park, London NW1 4RY

INDEX